So You Want to be a Healer

So You Want to be a Healer

Billy Roberts

AYNI
BOOKS

Winchester, UK
Washington, USA

First published by Ayni Books, 2012
Ayni Books is an imprint of John Hunt Publishing Ltd., Laurel House, Station Approach,
Alresford, Hants, SO24 9JH, UK
office1@o-books.net
www.o-books.com

For distributor details and how to order please visit the 'Ordering' section on our website.

Text copyright: Billy Roberts 2011

ISBN: 978 1 78099 166 5

A CIP catalogue record for this book is available from the British Library.

Design: Stuart Davies

Printed and bound by CPI Group (UK) Ltd, Croydon, CR0 4YY
Printed in the USA by Edwards Brothers Malloy

We operate a distinctive and ethical publishing philosophy in all
areas of our business, from our global network of authors to
production and worldwide distribution.

CONTENTS

INTRODUCTION

Although I have been mediumistically inclined since I was a child, in later life I was more interested in healing. In fact, even when I began working as a professional medium some time in 1980, I still ran a small healing clinic in Liverpool and at that time belonged to (N.F.S.H), The National Federation of Spiritual Healers. My deep interest in healing came about after I received healing from a Liverpool Healer by the name of Desmond Tierney, who really helped me overcome a serious illness. In fact, I owe a great deal to him, not only for the healing he gave me over a period of three years, but also for the things he taught me. He introduced me to various esoteric traditions and pointed me in the direction of the right books to read. With the realisation of just how powerfully effective healing actually was, Desmond Tierney helped me to become actively involved as a healer. This was in the mid-1970s, and after that introduction I began to seriously investigate healing in all its forms. I very quickly discovered that it did not in any way suggest that a person was a healer simply because he or she had set themselves up as a healing practitioner. In fact, I found out that many so-called healers were deluding themselves and just the same as in the world of mediums and psychics, anyone could set up a healing practice and become actively involved as a healer. In 1982-83 I established The Thought Workshop, the North West of England's very first Centre for Psychic and Spiritual Studies and Alternative Therapies. Nearly everyone I knew criticised me for this saying that it was far too adventurous, not to mention ambitious, especially as I had opened the centre in Rodney Street, the Harley Street of Liverpool. The centre was open 12 hours a day, 7 days a week, and was visited by people from all over the world. The most popular thing the centre had to offer was the healing, particularly the Spiritual Healing clinic which was always well attended. The healing courses were also very much in demand, and some of the students travelled great distances to take part.

As a small child I can recall my mother placing me close to the radio (the wireless as it was then called) so that I could touch it on the instruction of a well known healer who was transmitting his healing vibrations through the wireless airwaves. Although I have never found out the healer's name, in later years my mother informed me that he was a very well-known healer and that his name was known throughout the world. The transmission of healing through the radio just proves that actual physical contact is not necessary, and that it is certainly not restricted by distance. Some healers also send healing to the names of those in need entered in a so-called 'Healing Book', a popular and very effective way of sending healing to a sick person. This form of healing is often referred to as 'Absent Healing'. Spiritual Healing has never been confined to a specific religion or spiritual organisation. On the contrary, most religions have healing services in their churches, and from Shamanistic practitioners to the priests of Voodoo, healing is always found to be an integral part of their rituals and ceremonies.

SO YOU WANT TO BE A HEALER is intended for all those interested in all forms of healing, and consists of exercises, techniques and methods I have used in my workshops for nearly thirty years. Although I no longer practise as a healer, I do devote at least ten minutes of my day to the process of self-healing, something in which I totally believe.

CHAPTER ONE

THE MAGIC OF THE AURA

Everyone with an interest in healing, regardless of the method, should have some understanding of the human aura and the subtle anatomy. It is quite easy for a sceptic to dismiss the very suggestion that one individual can heal another, but the truth is that man's metaphysical powers have always been an integral part of his spiritual and psychological evolution.

From time immemorial the human aura has been depicted in many different ways, from the biblical account of Joseph's coat of many colours, to the halo painted by medieval artists around the heads of saints. Today though as well as being a metaphysical phenomenon, the aura is also a scientific fact, and is perhaps an indication that man's energies extend far beyond the confines of the visible spectrum.

In fact, the phenomenon of the aura has caused a great deal of controversy over the years, and has also been the topic for many debates amongst scientists and pseudo scientists, such as parapsychologists and paranormal researchers. Nonetheless, it still continues to fascinate and intrigue both sceptic and those with an interest in esoteric and metaphysical sciences. However, as to what the aura is exactly still remains a mystery even though many theories have been given as to its true nature. It is spoken of by mediums with some authority, even though what the majority actually see is only a minute part of an even greater whole. Even scientists agree that the human organism is an electromagnetic unit of immense power, appropriating, assimilating and releasing energy, and is also contained within its own spectrum of light and colour. Extensive studies of the human aura have found that it constantly changes and that it is greatly affected by diet, thought, mood and the overall condition of the health. Following extensive studies in the early fifties into the bioluminescence of the body, Russian scientists were convinced that they had discovered the 'key' to making an accurate diagnosis of disease, and concluded that all diseases were visible in the aura long before they became apparent in the body. Bioluminescence is the production and emission of light by a living organism, and is thought to be the result of a chemical reaction during which chemical energy is converted into light energy. This optical phenomenon is seen in some aquatic creatures, and in the human organism is an external indication as to the degree of internal balance or imbalance, whichever the case maybe. The scientists' extensive research into human biolumines-cence led them to postulate that there is also a Bio-plasma body interpenetrating the physical body. They further concluded that this Bio-plasma body was a sort of *etheric framework* or matrix on which the physical body is constructed, rather like the wire framework on which a sculptor moulds his clay. It appeared to the researchers that when the Bio-plasma body sustained damage as a consequence of inconsistent energy flow, a corresponding effect was produced in the overall condition of the physical body, manifesting as disease. The research was groundbreaking at the time and led to even further investigations into the metaphysical side of the human organism.

The first to photograph the aura were husband and wife team, Semyon and Valentina Kirlian whose crude apparatus enabled them to produce a monochrome image of the radiations of energy around the hands. Through their studies the Kirlians also concluded that disease manifested in the aura some considerable time before it became apparent in the physical body. The Kirlian's crude photographic device was in fact an inspiration to others working in the same field, and the Kirlian camera (as it was called) was later used as a diagnostic tool and was regarded as an innovation in the medical world at the time. Today, however, there are more sophisticated cameras capable of photographing the aura in its entirety and in full colour, as opposed to just photographing the energy around the hands. The extremely clearly defined coloured images produced by the more modern digital cameras today are even accompanied by a detailed computerised analysis, containing the holistic data of the individual to which the aura belongs. Even though a diagnosis of disease with the use of such means is today believed to be unreliable, the concept of the aura camera has opened up a whole new world where metaphysical man is concerned.

Sometime around 1920, Walter Kilner, a Radiologist at St Thomas' Hospital in London developed a unique method of making the aura visible. This involved two connecting blue tinted screens containing the dye dicyanin that enabled three distinct layers of the human aura to be seen by even a non-psychic person. Although Kilner had no knowledge at all of metaphysics, his observations with the use of his aura screen enabled him to detect illness long before it became apparent in the body. He published his finding in his bestselling book, *The Human Atmosphere*, now titled *The Aura*.

From a metaphysical point of view the human aura is also a sort of prehistoric radar device capable of detecting danger in the surrounding environment. It is seen to be more extensive at the back than it is at the front, but in a visually handicapped person, most probably to compensate for the absence of sight, it extends the same distance all round the body.

The aura is in fact best described as a vaporous mass of electromagnetic particles surrounding both animate and inanimate matter. However, the aura surrounding the human form is full of movement and colour as it extends some distance from the body, and really represents the degree of life and consciousness present.

The strides of a person taking a leisurely stroll through woodland are significantly affected if he or she is being watched.

The movement of the muscles of the legs are noticeably restricted, even though the walker is completely unaware that they are being observed. This is a clear indication that the electromagnetic impulses of the aura are able to 'detect' things in the environment even when they are invisible to the physical eye.

The aura of someone who is sick or just under the weather will always draw energy from the aura of a healthy person, clearly in an effort to be revitalised. This phenomenon is easily replicated in the following experiment which you may like to try:

- *Cut a fresh apple in two and remove the pips. Make sure they are the dark pips as opposed to white.*
- *Place two pips on a white piece of paper and just stare at them for a few moments.*
- *You will see a white to pale blue vaporous glow around them, moving in a clockwise motion.*

NEXT:

- *Place the pips in an envelope and leave them there for 24 hours.*
- *After this time, retrieve the pips from the envelope and place them once again on the white piece of paper, and see how the energy has changed. The glow will not seem as vibrant, and should appear fragmented, representing lack of vitality and disease.*
- *Now, place some fresh pips approximately half an inch away from the old pips and watch what happens.*
- *The energy from the old pips will appear to reach out to the fresh pips in a final effort to be revitalised, just like the aura of a sick person, drawing energy from a healthy one.*

The aura is truly a mystery and a phenomenon that has been recognised from time immemorial by all religious cultures. When we refer to someone who is glowing with happiness we often say

'She is in the pink', and when someone is jealous or envious, we might say 'She is green with envy'. 'Yellow' is a term frequently used to describe someone who is a coward, and we say 'red with anger' to describe someone's temper. All these colours represent the human temperament and mood swings, and once you are able to actually 'see' the aura, a whole new dimension opens up to you. I am always reminded of the story of the man who had died and was standing before God, proffering all the things he had done in life. God smiled at him, and said: *'My son, no need for your reports, I know you by the colour of your thoughts.'*

CHAPTER TWO

MAGNETIC AND PRANIC HEALING

Magnetism is active everywhere, and there is nothing new in it but the term. It is a paradox only to those who ridicule everything, and who attribute to the power of Satan whatever they are unable to explain.

Although Magnetic Healing is perhaps similar to Pranic healing, at least in the way they are administered, neither methods should be confused with spiritual healing which is a different concept altogether. This misconception is still harboured today by a lot of people who actually practise magnetic healing in the belief that they are administering spiritual healing.

Before we move any further it is necessary to give you an understanding of exactly what Prana is, so that you know the difference between this and magnetism. Prana is the subtle agent through which the life of the body is sustained. The more prana that enters and remains in the physical body, the higher the quality of life. A reduction in prana results in the lowering of your vitality, and ultimately deterioration in the quality of life. Where there is no prana, of course, there can be no life. Prana is the principle responsible for the integration of the cells into a whole, and so when it withdraws through the natural process of age, the body ultimately dies and disintegrates. So, you have to understand that prana has its own particular parts to play in the manifestation of life, apart from the obvious physiological function. Certain methods of healing involve the control and manipulation of prana, usually through a system of breathing techniques known as *Pranayama*, meaning the control of prana. However, some individuals naturally store large amounts of prana in their bodies, and when in their presence for any length of time, a sick person feels overwhelmed and invigorated. People who work on the land, such as farmers or enthusiastic gardeners usually store large amounts of prana in their nervous systems. Some athletes too, especially swimmers are able to store large amounts of prana in their bodies. Water is a conduit for prana, which is why it is very healthy to live by the sea or other expanses of water.

Magnetic or pranic healing involves the transmission of an individual's own energies, and while there are different theories as to how this process takes place it is an ability we all possess to a greater or lesser degree. Spiritual Healing involves a certain degree of attunement with the patient, and also a blending of the healer's mind with a *higher power* or the expansion of consciousness. In my experience Spiritual Healing necessitates some degree of spiritual attainment and discipline but very little technique, while the effectiveness of magnetic or pranic healing is primarily dependent on ability and technique.

In the seventeenth century, when the chemist and physician Van Helmont was writing, a Scotsman by the name of Maxwell was practising and teaching the art of magnetic healing. Although this was looked upon with some disdain by the church, Maxwell's belief in an all-pervading vital spirit that could be tapped into to heal the sick caught the imagination of his numerous devotees.

A similar idea became popular in 1734, when a priest by the name of Father Hehl propagated the idea of a 'Universal Fluid' that could be used to cure all manner of illnesses. Needless to say, Father Hehl was branded a heretic and was eventually driven from the church.

At the end of the eighteenth century, Friedrich Anton Mesmer, the innovator of Mesmerism, the forerunner to hypnotism, taught the radical and unconventional theory of *animal magnetism*. Initially, Mesmer was held in high esteem in

Vienna and Paris, and was looked upon as a sort of guru of his day. The Prussian government established a hospital devoted to the application of magnetic healing, and such was the interest in the subject that strict laws were introduced by various Continental governments to prevent anyone outside the medical profession from using magnetic treatments. Nonetheless, Mesmer and his idea eventually fell into disfavour, and some of his followers seized the opportunity to exploit the knowledge they had obtained from him, thus prostituting what they had learned. However, their interpretation of his teachings did give birth to new schools of thought centred primarily around the transference of energy.

HOW MAGNETIC HEALING AFFECTS THE AURA

Although pranic healing is far more effective when administered by a healthy person, someone who is unwell can facilitate the movement of prana in their own body for the sole purpose of healing themselves. The majority of those studying the subject agree that health problems manifest in the aura some considerable time before any symptoms actually become apparent in the physical body. However, to a sceptic this notion will probably seem absurd and regarded as far-fetched and fanciful. Nonetheless, scientific research has proved this to be a fact, and the use of such apparatus as the modern Kirlian camera has now substantiated the claims made by those researching this incredible phenomenon. Experiments with magnetic healing and the aura have proved conclusively that auric fragmentations can be corrected with as few as two treatments. Magnetic passes to the aura appear to polarise it, making it sharp and vibrant. When the aura is fragmented it can easily be infiltrated by psychic germs, thus lowering its resistance to physical as well as psychological disease. Auric fragmentations often occur as a result of poor diet, alcohol, nicotine and drug abuse, as well as wrong thinking. By holistically treating a fragmented aura, leakages may be sealed and the *whole* person grounded as a result. The process promotes a more balanced individual in body, mind and spirit, thus encouraging a more positive attitude to everyday life. Magnetic healing has a 'sweeping' effect upon the subtle anatomy and encourages a more consistent movement of prana through the meridians and nadis, the major and minor channels through which pranic energy flows.

The aura may also be looked upon as a sort of blueprint of the individual it represents, and contains all relevant data about the person's psychological, spiritual and physical make-up. A detailed analysis of the aura will enable you to create a complete profile of the individual's well-being. In other words, everything you need to know about a person is contained in his or her personal energy field and may be accessed at any time.

Another effective way of polarising the aura is with the use of metal magnets. Because the aura extends some distance from the body, it is not necessary to actually make physical contact with the person. The following section explains how the magnetic procedure should be implemented. Metal magnets come in various strengths, and today small and extremely powerful healing magnets are available at specialist dealers. The effect these powerful magnets have on the aura is quite remarkable, and so the length of time they are used in any one treatment should be kept to a minimum.

THE PROCESS OF MAGNETIC HEALING

For the magnetic treatment you will require two metal magnets, large enough to hold comfortably in the hands.

- *Take a magnet in each hand, and begin by holding them above the head of your seated patient, about two inches from the head and about three inches from each other.*
- *Begin the treatment by slowly moving the magnets in opposite directions around the sides of the person's body, working*

downwards and shaking your hands slightly as they move.

- *Take time with the treatment, and when you have reached the hip area follow the same route back up to the top of the head. Repeat this process three or four times.*
- *Following the same procedure as before, this time move one magnet down the back of your patient and one down the front, again taking time with the treatment.*

Remember, although you are treating the subtle energies of the person's aura you are actually using the magnetic properties of two solid objects, therefore no visualisation or mental imagery are necessary for positive results to be achieved.

Once the treatment has been concluded the patient should drink a glass or two of water to ensure that the body is fully hydrated. This facilitates the healing process and encourages the movement of prana in the body on the conclusion of the magnetic treatment. Because the person's aura has been polarised it is quite normal for them to feel light headed or even slightly disorientated. However, this should only last until the magnetic polarisation process has taken effect, and everything should be back to normal within five minutes. In any case, it is also an integral part of the treatment to reassure the patient, perhaps by talking them through some gentle relaxation.

It is not necessary to apply the treatment to the entire body, as once the magnetic waves infiltrate the upper part of the aura the whole energy field will be affected within minutes.

MAGNETISING YOUR OWN AURA

There are various ways of infusing your own aura with vitality, one of which is the self-magnetising process. This is an extremely simple procedure again involving the use of two metal magnets, one held in each hand.

- *Sit quietly on a straight backed chair, holding a magnet in each hand.*

- *Holding the magnets gently on your lap, close your eyes and breathe rhythmically, ensuring that the inhalations and exhalation are evenly spaced.*
- *When you feel quite relaxed and your mind is quiet, place one hand (holding the magnetic) on top of the head, and the other hand (holding the other magnet) at the base of your spine.*
- *Remain in this position until the temperature in either hand changes, at which point, move the hand on top of your head to the base of your spine, and the hand on the base of your spine to the top of your head, and repeat the same process.*
- *Repeat this procedure five or six times, alternating the positions of the hands, at the same time relaxing as completely as you possibly can.*

This self-magnetising process is ideal for stabilising your aura and precipitating the movement of prana through it, and is particularly effective when you are feeling tired or simply under the weather. By guiding your patient through the magnetic process the same method maybe used to administer the same treatment during your healing practise.

Healing magnets may also be used to effectively re-align and polarise the chakra system in the following way. For this treatment you will require seven small healing magnets.

- *Secure your patient in a comfortable horizontal position, ensuring that he or she is totally relaxed with their eyes closed and their head resting on a pillow.*
- *Corresponding with the seven major chakras, place the magnets strategically along his or her body, beginning with the forehead and concluding with the lowest part of the abdomen.*
- *Talk the person through some gentle relaxation and help them to visualise intense white light moving through the subtle channels, from magnet to magnet.*

- *Continue this for no longer than 6 to 8 minutes then remove the magnets, allowing your patient to remain in that position for a further five minutes.*
- *On the conclusion of the treatment the patient should sit in a comfortable chair and drink a glass of water.*

This is an extremely powerful treatment that will invigorate and revitalise the chakra system. Results are usually seen very quickly and really do have a long-lasting effect.

CHAPTER THREE

HEALING WITH PRANA

Although prana is in the air that we breathe, it is not the air itself. Prana is not matter but is found working through all forms of matter. Although it is prevalent in water, it is not the water itself. As previously stated water is a conduit of prana, and air and water combined create an extremely powerful healing agent, which is why in the old days the doctor always suggested a trip to certain seaside resorts to aid recovery from illness.

Although water has its own part to play in the conveyance of prana around the physical body, before it is actually consumed it can be either charged or infused with even more streams of prana, thus encouraging a more powerful presence of the force during the revitalisation process.

The pranic vitality in water may be greatly increased by using the vibrations of colour as a means of amplification. This method was in fact used by the ancient Egyptians who knew about the harmonics of colour and used chrometherapy to treat all manner of diseases of both the body and the mind.

The ancient Egyptian practitioners of colour therapy would use different coloured gauze which they would fix across an opening on the roof to filter the sun's rays. For an example, should the patient be lethargic perhaps as a consequence of depression, a blue filter would be used initially, followed by a green one. Blue is an excellent colour for restoring the body's vitality, and green has a harmonising effect upon the whole person. The treatment would then be concluded with a red filter, thus infusing the patient's body with energy and vitality. Because the vibrations of red can cause anxiety and anger in an individual who is exposed to it for too long, the red filter was only used until the patient's pallor became rosy. A full colour treatment chart will be given at the end of this chapter.

For this method you will need to have several A4 sheets of coloured acetate, each one in a colour of the spectrum. Alternatively, for ease, several coloured beakers (preferably glass but not essential) may be used.

COLOUR TREATMENT

- *Make a tube out of each piece of coloured acetate, ensuring that the circumference is wide enough for them to fit over a drinking glass, and then either secure each one with sellotape or staple them. (Unless of course drinking glasses are used.)*
- *Simply select the colour required, slip it over a glass of water and place it on the window ledge in the bright sunlight. Allow it to remain there for a couple of hours. Once the water is fully charged, it can either be kept in the fridge until required, or put through the following process before being consumed.*
- *Pour the water from one drinking vessel to another, over and over again until the water almost comes 'alive'. This pouring process 'wakens' the prana in the water, encouraging its potency ready to be drunk.*
- *As well as a noticeable difference in the taste of the water, you should also experience a gradual feeling of elation and overall feeling of well-being. Water charged in this way has a holistic effect upon the drinker and is an extremely effective way of complementing any treatment with conventional medicine.*

As I have already explained, prana is in the air that we breathe and can be controlled by a system of breathing techniques known as Pranayama, the control of prana. Using controlled breathing it is possible to encourage more prana to enter and remain in the body, and with the help of a little visualisation the in-flowing prana maybe directed to any part of the body where healing is needed. Prana can also be controlled sufficiently for it to be directed towards another person who you know is in need of healing.

Although there are many degrees of Pranayama breathing techniques, the most effective one for the transmission of prana either for the process of self-healing, or for the purpose of healing somebody else, is also the easiest to master.

MEASURED BREATHING – PRANAYAMA I

- *The rhythmic time of breathing is based on the counting of pulse units. The units of inhalation and exhalation in this case should always be the same, whilst the units of retention and between breaths should be one half the number of inhalation and exhalation.*

- *Sit comfortably on a straight back chair, ensuring that the chest, neck and head are as nearly in a straight line as possible, with the shoulders thrown slightly back and the hands resting, palms down on the lap.*

- *Until you have mastered the art of measured breathing, and have become more proficient at the technique, initially you should breathe to the count of 6/3.*

- *Before beginning the process of rhythmic breathing you should spend a few moments making the mind quiet and relaxing with your eyes closed.*

- *Make sure that when you breathe in that your stomach rises, and when you breathe out that it falls, ensuring that the inhalations and exhalations are evenly spaced all through the breathing process.*

- *When you feel quite relaxed and ready to begin, ascertain your normal heartbeat by placing your fingers on your pulse and counting 1,2,3,4,5,6; 1,2,3,4,5,6, and so on.*

- *Once the rhythm has been fully established in your mind, begin by slowly inhaling a complete breath for the count of six, hold it for the count of three, exhale for the count of six, count three between breaths, and so on. You should in fact continue this for around ten minutes, more if you feel inclined. Remember not to strain it or make it a labour, as this only defeats the object of the exercise and dissipates the force needlessly. Apart from that there is the danger of over-breathing.*

PRANAYAMA 2

The previous exercise encourages an increase of prana in the body, and the regulated breathing helps its retention and ultimate circulation through the subtle channels. Prana can also be greatly influenced by visualisation and may be brought under the control of the image-making faculty of the brain. It can also be mentally infused with colour and then discharged for a particular purpose, either to encourage someone back to good health, or to influence another person's mind. A note of caution here: should it be used for selfish reasons, or to influence another person against their will, you should be prepared for the consequences. Remember, *Curses and blessings come home to roost* - like will always attract like! This is the law of attraction which is both right and just. When using any techniques to influence other people for either good or ill, one should always adhere to a code of ethics and never do to others anything that you would not wish others to do to you.

- *As before, sit comfortably on a straight back chair, and with your eyes closed commence by making the mind quite. Inhale a complete breath, allowing your tummy to rise, and as you breathe out allow it to fall. This breathing in itself relaxes the body and makes the mind quiet in preparation for the exercise.*
- *When you are perfectly relaxed, with your eyes still closed, place your fingertips gently on your solar plexus, the area of the abdomen just below the ribcage.*
- *As you breath-in slowly, imagine streams of intense white light*

being drawn in through your nostrils, into your lungs and then into your solar plexus.

- *When your breath is complete, hold it, and then mentally see the white light in your fingertips, which should slowly be transferred to your forehead.*
- *On the exhalation, allow the white light to stream from your fingertips into your head, filling it completely with the intense white energy.*
- *When the breath has been fully expelled, hold it, and slowly return your fingertips to your solar plexus and repeat the exercise.*
- *Spend at least ten to fifteen minutes on the exercise, or until you feel your hands and forehead tingling with vitality.*

The object of this particular exercise is to increase the flow of prana in your body, as well as to stimulate and revitalise the brain and nerve plexuses. It is an effective way of easing tension and curing headaches but can also be used to alleviate pain in any part of the body. Equally, prana can also be transferred to another person using the same breathing and visualisation process.

- *Simply stand behind your seated patient, with your fingertips placed gently on your solar plexus, and breathe rhythmically for a few moments, thus establishing your connection with the person you are treating.*
- *As before, visualise the streams of prana as intense white light, flowing into your solar plexus with the in-coming breath, and when your breath is complete, transfer your fingertips to the top of your patient's head, as opposed to your own forehead, and then breathe the intense white light out through your fingertips into them.*
- *Remember, as mental interaction is an integral part of the exercise, visualisation is vitally important and should therefore*

be maintained constantly throughout the healing treatment.

In all eastern esoteric traditions, prana is the word used to describe *all* energy in the universe. It is believed to be the principle responsible for animation, and when prana withdraws from the body, through the natural process of age, the movement of our limbs is impaired and our mobility is greatly affected. By increasing the amounts of prana coming into the body it is possible to increase our longevity, maintaining our youthfulness and vitality.

One of the oldest methods of pranic healing is termed the 'blowing method,' and although it is not really the most hygienic of healing methods, it is one of the most effective, particularly when applied to our dog or cat.

For this method of pranic healing you will require a piece of white gauze or very thin white linen.

With this method of healing it is not necessary to actually apply the pranic treatment directly to the affected area of the body. When pranic healing is administered to the top of the head or even to the back of the neck (in human or animal) it is then quickly and efficiently absorbed and automatically drawn to the area of the body where it is most needed.

This particular treatment is holistic and is extremely effective on all illnesses, but especially when pain or inflammation is experienced. It also appears to encourage recovery from depression and other nervous or psychological illnesses.

Because of the nature of this type of treatment, it should really only be applied to family members, for obvious reasons.

PRANIC TREATMENT

- *Make certain that the patient is seated in a comfortable position, preferably on a chair where easy access can be gained to his or her back.*

- *Before beginning the treatment talk the patient through some simple relaxation, ensuring that he or she is fully prepared for what is going to happen.*
- *Place the piece of linen/gauze on top of the patient's head and allow it to remain there for a few moments.*
- *Inhale a complete breath, and then placing your mouth as close to the piece of cloth as possible, simply blow gently through it until all the breath has been fully expelled.*
- *Repeat this process for about five minutes before resting.*
- *This initial part of the pranic treatment is to establish contact with the patient, as well as to encourage heat in the top of their head.*
- *For the next part of the treatment you will need to involve some visualisation. Remember, prana can be mentally infused with any colour that you feel is appropriate for the treatment. When making the selection you would be wise to always be guided by instinct. As long as you remember the potency of the individual colours and how they affect the body, positive results will be experienced very quickly.*
- *Before beginning the blowing treatment, spend a few moments mentally allowing the chosen colour to be fully established in your mind. When you feel ready, inhale a complete breath and simply blow gently through the piece of cloth, at the same time imagining the out-flowing breath infused with the colour of your choice.*
- *When the breath has been fully exhaled, repeat the whole process immediately, once again fully discharging the colour with the out-flowing breath. The treatment should be maintained for no longer than ten minutes or until such time that the patient appears uncomfortable or restless.*

COLOUR CHART FOR THE PURPOSE OF PRANIC HEALING COLOUR AND CONDITIONS:

RED – *Anaemia; hyperthermia; lethargy;*

ORANGE: *Eczema; lack of energy; renal problems; bronchitis and asthma.*

YELLOW: *Constipation; gallbladder problems; lack of energy.*

GREEN: *Heart and lung problems; nervous disorders; depression; holistic treatment.*

BLUE: *Painful and inflammatory conditions. Anxiety and depression: high temperature; pneumonia and other bronchial conditions.*

INDIGO: *Lack of concentration: poor memory; depression and grief.*

VIOLET: *All painful and inflammatory conditions; all serious blood conditions. Holistic effect upon the person.*

CHAPTER FOUR

SCIENCE AND THE SUBTLE ANATOMY

As I have already said in a previous chapter, even science agrees that the human organism is an electromagnetic unit of immense power, contained within its own spectrum of colour and light. Although the human aura has been extensively covered in a previous chapter, as we are discussing the subtle anatomy it is necessary to touch upon it again very briefly. The electromagnetic field – the aura, also interpenetrates the physical body and reaches out to integrate with other energies. To ensure that the immense power generated by the electromagnetic field of the body is stabilised, a system of etheric channels can be found permeating the entire subtle anatomy. Strategically connected to these channels, and looking like small flowers, whose petals increase as they ascend the spine, are seven transformer-like vortices called chakras. The word 'chakra' means wheel or circle, obviously to describe the fact that they rotate and look to all intents and purposes like coloured whirlpools of energy, each with a higher degree of vibration than the one below it. It is the primary function of the seven major chakras to control the inflowing prana, and to modulate and evenly distribute it throughout the body, thereby maintaining the equilibrium of body, mind and spirit. There are in fact hundreds of minor chakras permeating the entire subtle anatomy, each one performing its own individual function in the relentless process of maintaining balance and harmony on all levels of existence. However, the seven major chakras are considered primary, and these are to be found across the surface of the etheric tract in the spinal column. These chakras are in fact connected to the endocrine glands and nerve plexuses through an extensive system of channels called 'nadis'. The word Nadi means 'nerve', only at a more subtle level, and it is along these Nadis that prana flows constantly, from the chakras to the organs of the physical body. Apart from everything else, each individual major chakra is responsible for the evolution of spiritual consciousness at its corresponding level, and collectively they maintain balance in the individual's life.

Although all seven major chakras are potentially present at birth, it normally takes a full seven years for the entire chakra system to fully evolve. When a child emerges from its mother's womb only one chakra is fully active – the base chakra at the bottom of the spine. This controls the autonomic nervous system, supervising the involuntary functioning of the body, and is known as *Muladhara* in Sanskrit. The consciousness of a newborn baby is focused on the base chakra for the first 12 months of its life, after which time the second chakra begins to unfold, and so on, until the seven chakras are fully formed at the age of seven. It is usually during this time that the consciousness of the newborn baby becomes accustomed to its new environment. Some schools of thought believe that the seven major chakras are also like 'cosmic banks', and contain the experience of all previous incarnations. This could account for the fact why some children appear to be far more advanced and psychically aware than others, and some even have memories of having lived in this world before. It has been suggested that up until the age of seven, the majority of children have a perfect memory of life before they were born. However, all this quickly changes when his or her parents begin the psychological process of education and chastisement. As a result of this parental programming the vibratory movement of the individual chakras changes completely, and then the child forgets from whence it came.

Having explored the spiritual role of the subtle anatomy we can now take a look at the part it plays where the holistic health is concerned.

In the same way that an engine of a car can develop faults, impairing its performance, so too can the subtle anatomy develop problems. These problems are usually connected to the restriction of energy movement through the nadis and meridians, and usually occur as a result of wrong thinking, stress and poor diet. The nadis and meridians develop blockages preventing energy from moving freely along them, and as a consequence health problems are created in the body. An acupuncturist or reflexologist can usually alleviate these problems quite easily. The acupuncturist will insert fine needles in strategic sites, corresponding to the appropriate channels, across the surface of the skin. These stimulate and encourage the energy to flow freely once again, thus alleviating the problem. Reflexology works on the premise that all the channels may be located in the feet, and blockages thus occur when the energy crystallises at significant sites on the soles of the feet. Gentle manipulation of strategic points in the feet helps to breakdown the crystallised energy, thereby encouraging it to flow freely once again, thus curing the health problem. There is no doubt that both these complementary practises are effective and do work at a subtle level. Although I have never been treated by an acupuncturist I have been treated by a reflexologist and did feel incredibly well after it.

Both Magnetic and pranic treatments encourage balance in the subtle anatomy, and when administered on a fairly regular basis can help a diseased body to heal itself. Although a minority of diehard scientists dismiss the majority of alternative healing treatments as no more than hokum, there is an ever increasing majority who believe in it sufficiently to investigate it further.

In 1903 after a sojourn in a Tibetan monastery, neuroscientist, Ivan Tutinsky from Moscow University, became so fascinated in the functioning of the pineal gland, the pine-shaped gland deep within the brain, that he compromised his professional integrity by devoting seven years of his life to making a detailed analysis of it. Although Tutinsky was ridiculed by his peers, he wanted desperately to know why the Tibetan masters held the pineal gland in such a high esteem, and believed that it was responsible for the manifestation of all of man's supernatural abilities. Although Tutinsky took pains to avoid the word 'psychic', he was intrigued and wanted to know why some people, especially children, possessed such unusual *powers* and others did not. At the end of Tutinsky's seven year research, he concluded that the pineal gland in children was in fact larger than in an adult, and marginally more developed in a female than in a male. Furthermore, he discovered that the pineal gland in those who exhibited supernatural abilities was considerably larger than those with no such abilities. Tutinsky was in no doubt that the pineal gland radiated magnetic waves and was most certainly responsible for the manifestation of unusual mental abilities. Today this is all common knowledge, and even more research has been conducted into the functioning of the brain when paranormal skills are present.

More recent studies into the brain and how it functions have shed even more light on the great mystery of why we have psychic experiences at all.

Contained within the boney box of the skull is a complex mass of nerve cells called neurons and these are assisted by other cells known as neuroglia. The majority of these trillions of cells are contained within a layer of grey matter called the cerebral cortex, which neurologists believe to be the centre of consciousness and thought. The cells across this area responsible for the processing of data received from the external world by means of our five senses. Once processed, the data are then transferred to the internal regions of the cerebral cortex. Individuality is then created once the memory data have joined together with various other pieces of information from other parts of the brain, to form feelings, thoughts, images and ideas.

Although the information is processed by the brain's neurons through electrical impulses, how exactly these impulses become thoughts and feelings is still a mystery to those researching in the field of neuroscience. One interesting scientific conclusion is that we have three brains as opposed to one, each one vastly different from the others in both structure and function. However, even though the three brains all appear significantly different, there is some sort of correspondence between them.

The first and oldest of the three brains is known as the reptilian brain and is responsible for our survival instincts, the hunter and fighter in us, and most probably the lower passions and emotions. The limbic system, the second part of the brain, is an interconnected system of brain nuclei and is associated with basic needs and emotions; for example, hunger, pain, pleasure, sexual desire and instinctive motivation. This is located in the inner wall of each cerebral hemisphere and includes the brain system concerned with the sense of smell. The most recently evolved and third part of the brain is the cerebral cortex, believed to represent the clear divide between humans and animals, as the saying goes: 'Man knows, the animal knows, but man knows that he knows'. This is the reasoning part of the brain and the part that enables us to form ideas, create culture and learn new concepts.

Some psychologists believe that the human is in fact a twofold being consisting of the *ego* or real self, as in Eastern philosophy, and an *intuitive self*. Most psychologists believe that the ego is situated in the cerebral cortex, the newest part of the brain, and the intuitive self is associated more with the oldest part of the brain, which is referred to as the cerebellum, the unconscious, and the part of the brain responsible for dreams. In fact, some believe that the cerebellum is also responsible for paranormal experiences and is that part of the brain that controls the so-called 'trance' state. However, there are conflicting theories about this concept, and others researching the subject of the function of the brain believe that the cerebral cortex, in the right hemisphere of the brain, is in fact where psychic experiences originate.

Scientists in America also believe that they have identified the module in the brain in which God exists, and that many people suffering from temporal lobe epilepsy frequently have spiritual experiences during an epileptic seizure. Scientists all over the world are today endeavouring to understand the complexities of the brain, and to find out why many people claim to have paranormal experiences. Tests have shown that the electrical circuitry in the brain of a healer, psychic or medium is somehow significantly interrupted when he or she is demonstrating their ability, and a significant fluctuation in brainwave activity is also apparent when monitored by an electroencephalograph (EEG). Experiments were conducted using a computerised aura camera, whilst a healer was administering his treatment, at the same time as being connected to an EEG. The results revealed an obvious correspondence of activity between the graph of the EEG and the computerised imagery of the aura camera, leaving very little doubt that brain activity did most definitely affect the polarity of the healer's aura. However, some working in the field of metaphysics believe that it could be the other way round, and that it may be the fluctuation in auric polarity that affects the electrical activity in the brain. Whatever the conclusions, as I have previously said the brains of those with a propensity towards paranormal abilities are far from normal, and significant changes most definitely do occur in the overall activity of the brain's electrical circuitry when they are demonstrating their skills.

It is not clear whether the mind exerts an influence over the individual chakras, or whether it is the other way round. However, it is certain that the chakras do influence and motivate an individual in his or her aspirations, whether spiritual or otherwise. It is wrongly assumed that chakras only work towards a person's spiritual development, when in actual fact they encourage the consciousness of all the individual's endeavours, whatever they are. As a musician I can teach twenty people the fundamental principles of the guitar, but perhaps only one or two will possess the potential to become sufficiently proficient to play the instrument to a professional standard. One may have aspirations towards healing the sick, and may have even acquired all the knowledge of the various healing techniques, however, should the potential not be present in the appropriate chakra – in this case, the heart chakra (known as Anahata) then development of a healing skill will be very limited. The development of any paranormal ability requires far more than knowledge and good intentions, even though spiritual development is available to everyone.

CHAKRAS AND THEIR ANATOMICAL POSITIONS

Sahasrara	*The Crown of the Head*
Ajna	*Brow Centre (Third Eye)*
Vishudda	*Throat (Thyroid)*
Anahata	*Heart*
Manipura	*Solar Plexus*
Svadisthana	*Sacrum*
Muladhara	*Root (Base of spine.)*

CHAPTER FIVE

TRANSCENDENTAL HEALING

The need to heal is deeply woven into our biological makeup and is an integral part of our instinctive nature. A mother comforts her child when it has fallen over, and will lovingly sooth away the discomfort by gently rubbing the painful knee. Within moments the child recovers and carries on playing without giving any more thought to the bruising on its knee. A caring nurse will gently reassure the sick patient with a warm hand and softly spoken words. We've all experienced healing at some time in our lives, whether it has been in our mother's loving arms, or from the kind words of a teacher at school. But, you must have noticed that not all people have this ability, and that a minority exude anything but healing. In fact, some people appear cold and unfriendly, and others appear to send out strong signals warning us not to come too close, perhaps because he or she is afraid to show any signs of warmth or love. However, some individuals are so gentle and loving that it's always a pleasure to meet them to stop for a little chat on the High Street. You may have on the odd occasion been feeling a little miserable and under the weather when you bumped into the elderly lady from down the street. She always seems to be smiling and sufficiently astute to see that all is not well with you. A few moments spent in the old lady's company is all that is required to put the smile back on your face and a spring in your steps. So, what it is about such people who seem to possess that certain 'something' that they always unconsciously pass on to others? Whatever it is it is what makes a nurse caring and good at her job, and a doctor sufficiently observant to 'know' you are unwell without you having to tell him your symptoms. Without this certain 'something' healing cannot transpire between the healer and the patient. Simply thinking that you've got what it takes to be a healer when you have not is just being self-deluded and can very often do more harm than good, simply by filling a sick person with false hope. I have seen this happen so many times in the field of healing. Today it is far too easy for someone to embark upon the path of healing and to become a member of some healing organisation. After serving the required probationary period, a certificate is awarded to endorse that he or she is a qualified healer. Perhaps it's not always as easy as that, but I am sure you get the gist of what I am saying.

All cultures and religious and philosophical traditions have had their healers, highly respected individuals in the community, who would be consulted for all manner of problems. It would seem that spirituality was not always a prerequisite of the healer, who would very often exploit their position and abuse the vulnerability of those who consulted them. An example of this was the monk Grigori Yefimovich Rasputin. He was sometimes referred to as either the 'Mad Monk' or the 'Black Monk', and was known to be a debauched religious charlatan, who exploited his healing powers and his abilities as a seer and self-confessed prophet. Nobody can dispute Rasputin's powers which he allegedly received after he had a vision of the Virgin Mary. Rasputin is perhaps proof that supernatural abilities are not dependent on spirituality, or even belief in God or any Divine power. Rasputin allegedly possessed immense power and was able to hypnotise and cure the sick of all manner of maladies. I'm sure that many reading this chapter will think using Rasputin as an example is perhaps a little extreme. Nonetheless, he just proves the point I am making, and throughout antiquity there have been many other healers just like him.

Many ancient seers and healers used either herbal narcotics or hallucinogenic substances to bring about altered states of consciousness. Even though this is most certainly not recommended it was their belief that hallucinogens would enable them to access other dimensions. Once an altered state of consciousness had been achieved, the healer would be able to diagnose what was wrong with the sick person, and with the help of a metaphysical, transcendental power, healing could then be administered. Although the methods were a little extreme to say the least, many people were successfully healed in this way.

Although many ancient healers followed the more traditional route through meditation and other transcendental disciplines, a minority chose the quicker and more dangerous methods of imbibing hallucinogens. The practise of imbibing hallucinogenic substances to produce transcendental states was extremely popular in certain religious cultures, who used the relied upon hallucinogens to bring them closer to God and the realms of the souls of their dead ancestors. The hallucinogens were derived from a variety of naturally occurring plants, from Amanita Muscaria, the so-called 'Magical Mushroom', used in Shamanic healing rituals, to Mescaline, extracted from the button-shaped nodules of the Mexican Peyote spineless cactus, frequently used by the Aztec priests during their transcendental healing sessions. Another was Psilocybin, a crystalline hallucinogen, also obtained from the so-called 'Sacred Mushroom' used by a mystical sect known as the 'Mushroom People,' whose whole spiritual philosophy was centred around the hallucinogenic properties of the mushroom. In fact, hallucinogens have been an integral part of many spiritual cultures, and some even referred to the hallucinogenic substances they used as the 'Nectar of the Gods.'

Whilst there can be no doubt that the hallucinogens did produce altered states of consciousness, some individuals never came out of the transcendental experience and the psychological damage produced a psychosis, making the user believe that he was actually a divine being. As a consequence, hallucinogens were only used by spiritually qualified individuals who imbibed the mind-altering substance when they needed to call upon the higher powers of the cosmos. As well as anything else, hallucinogens greatly affected the pineal gland by increasing its potency and causing the release of even more melatonin into the brain. Research has shown that there is a crystalline deposit around the pineal gland, deep within the brain, encouraging an increase in electromagnetic waves. As discussed in an earlier chapter, the pineal gland is considered to be responsible for all transcendental or spiritual abilities, and its actual size appears to determine the degree and depth of the ability.

There are in fact meditation techniques specifically designed for the cultivation of healing skills. However, as previously stated, a healing skill can only be developed if the potential is there in the first place. It must also be said that many people possess a great deal of healing potential but lack the desire to do anything with it. This is a great shame, and I am sure that there are people in the world who are completely unaware that they do possess incredible healing abilities and whose circumstances prevent them from developing them further.

Whether you have aspirations to developing a healing ability you are certain you possess, or simply have a desire to use the power you possess to heal yourself, is really immaterial, as the same methods are used in all cases.

First of all, the ultimate development of any healing ability has to be for a reason, and preferably not a selfish one. Should you secretly harbour the desire to become a healer for the sake of your ego, or for the adulation and fame, then I would reconsider the whole thing. The lives of all those who have exploited their abilities for selfish reasons have nearly all come to tragic ends. I have used Rasputin as one example, but there have been many, many more throughout history.

In all cases of the development of healing powers, meditation has to be the most effective method. The first thing to fix firmly in your mind is the fact that there is a power that you can call upon and control through rhythmic breathing, and that this power can be discharged into another person. The amazing thing about pranic energy is the fact that one can discharge it to a person without having any physical contact with them. In an earlier chapter I explained how it can be infused with colour for the purpose of healing. Using a process termed 'Distant Healing', one can discharge the healing power with such force, that it is able to reach a sick person on the other side of the world, distance no object.

Concentrations of energy may be created with a specific mission in mind, and once given the mental command, it can be then sent forth in the direction of the person for whom the healing is intended. The ancient Egyptians used the same principles to mentally create *Thought Forms* – invisible entities to protect the tombs of their great kings. Many of these powerful Thought Forms are still there today, silently watching over the as yet undiscovered burial chambers of ancient Egyptian nobility. Thought Forms can either be created unknowingly by an individual with sufficient power, or consciously with a specific intention in mind. Even though no physical contact is required it is still nonetheless an extremely powerful form of healing, and one that should at all times be treated with respect.

CHAPTER SIX

THE PRINCIPLES OF DISTANT HEALING

It is known to anyone with an understanding of the fundamental principles of Thought Dynamics, that an individual on the other side of the world can be psychologically influenced without them having any knowledge of what is happening. The concept of Distant Healing is by no means new and the process has been used by many philosophical and religious traditions, and even today is still used by many Spiritualist and other practising healers.

PREPARTION:

- *Sit comfortably, preferably on a chair with a straight back, ensuring that your legs are not crossed and your feet are on the floor, side by side.*
- *Make sure that your neck and head are as nearly in a straight line as possible, with your shoulders thrown slightly back and your hands resting lightly on your lap with your eyes closed.*
- *Breathe rhythmically until the rhythm is fully established, ensuring that the inhalations and exhalations are evenly spaced.*
- *At this point make no attempt to empty your mind, but simply allow the thoughts to come and go, at the same time resisting the temptation to think of anything in particular.*
- *Remain like this for at least ten minutes, and then allow your mind to drift from your breathing until you become almost unconscious of it.*
- *Allow your senses to mentally scan your surroundings, and endeavour to be totally aware of everything around you.*
- *Be aware of every sound, every fragrance, and even feel the*

pressure of the air around against your skin. In other words, be totally aware of where you are, and who you are.

- *Allow all sensations of smell, sound and feeling to be processed by all your senses, and for a moment try to become totally detached from your body, to the extent that you feel that you could leave your body at any time.*
- *Try to remain as still as possible, and then slowly be aware of your breathing again. As you breathe in allow your stomach to rise, and when you breathe out allow it to fall. In fact, allow this rhythm to be maintained whilst your body remains perfectly still.*
- *Allow this exercise to slowly fade, and when you feel you are ready open your eyes and sit there for a few minutes longer whilst gathering your thoughts.*

It is quite normal to feel slightly disorientated for a few moments, but this should clear very quickly. Before attempting the following exercise you should repeat the preparation process each day for at least a week. All meditation periods should commence and conclude with some rhythmic breathing, to clear the mind and sharpen the senses.

THE FIRST STEP TO CREATING A THOUGHT FORM

Before beginning to create the Thought Form you should spend a few minutes contemplating on the person to whom it is to be sent. Remember, because you have created it the Thought Form will possess the same power you yourself possess, and once released it will carry all that power, in the blinking of an eye, directly to the person for whom it is intended. Look upon the Thought Form as a missile and your mind as the missile launcher.

- *Because of the sensitive nature of this process, before beginning it would be a good idea if you were to create a sacred space, either in a specially prepared corner of the garden, or just in a specifi-cally selected part of a room in your home.*

- *Creating a thought form in this way requires total concentration and focus, and so it sometimes helps to place a lighted candle in front of you, about three feet away, and as close to eye level as possible. Also, to help create the correct ambience it helps to burn some pleasant incense.*
- *Light the candle and spend a few minutes gazing at the tip of the flame. Think of nothing in particular, but at the same time make no attempt to prevent the thoughts from passing through your consciousness, as this merely defeats the object of the whole exercise.*
- *Begin to breathe rhythmically, ensuring that the inhalations and exhalations are evenly spaced, and that you do not strain it or make it a labour.*
- *Allow your thoughts to drift away from the flame, but at the same time ensuring that your eyes are still fixed on the tip of it, almost as though you are daydreaming.*
- *Continue this mental process for ten minutes, or for as long as is comfortable, and then allow the image of the person who is to receive the healing to gradually come into your mind. Now, slowly close your eyes.*
- *The after image of the flame of the candle will soon appear in your mind's eye. Allow this to persist whilst focusing on the image of the person who is to receive the healing.*
- *Focus on the person for as long as the after-image of the flame persists in your mind, and when this fades make every effort to make his or her image as clear as possible.*
- *See the person glowing with health and vitality. Hold this image for a further five minutes, and then breathe-in deeply, and when you breathe out allow it all to fade from your mind.*
- *Spend a further five minutes just imbibing the peace and quiet. And then, when you feel ready open your eyes.*

Although healing in this way is very often spontaneous, actually creating the *Thought Form* takes time, patience and determination. In order for the *Thought Form* to be fully activated, you will need to retreat to your *Sacred Space* at least once a day, more if time permits. Remember, you are endeavouring to create a concentrated force that will perform in your absence; therefore you must slowly empower it by systematically infusing it with all the power of your *will*. Once created and released, you must be certain that it is discharged with the correct intentions – in this case to heal. Of course Thought Forms can be created for many different reasons; their power and force is solely dependent upon you. For this reason you must approach the whole mental process with great respect, always remembering the precept: *'Curses and Blessings Come Home to Roost!'* Should you ever create a *Thought Form* with the sole intention of inflicting harm on another person, it will rebound from them and return immediately to you, gathering force from the impact! This is the Law of Attraction; a law which is both right and *just!*

THE DYNAMICS OF THOUGHT

You are the architect of your own destiny by the way you think. This precept is an integral part of esoteric philosophy, and *what you are is a reflection of how you think* should always be borne in mind when endeavouring to follow a spiritual path. Thoughts crystallise into habit, and habit eventually solidifies into circumstances. It is easier to change the way you think than it is to change your circumstances. Given that your thoughts form the very foundation of your circumstances, you can prepare your future circumstances now by the way you think.

The various waves of thought produced and discharged by each individual form thought strata in the psychic space, in very much the same way that clouds form groups in the atmosphere. But this does not mean that each stratum of thought occupies a section of space to the exclusion of all other thought clouds. On the contrary, the particles of thought of which the clouds are created are of different degrees of vibration; and so the same space may be filled with thought matter of a trillion kinds, passing freely and interpenetrating each other without interference. Each particle of thought draws to itself thought matter of a similar kind. Districts, towns, cities and nations are permeated by the thoughts of those who live or have lived throughout time, and these influence the minds of all those who come within their radiance. This in fact is one of the fundamental principles of Quantum physics, and is a law that is in constant operation all through our lives. In a similar way old houses are affected by the same phenomenon. The bricks and mortar structure of old buildings are in fact impregnated by the thoughts, feelings and emotions of all those who have lived within their confines. The electromagnetic atmosphere of a building is able to 'record' images and sounds, in much the same way as the process of recording images and sounds on video and audio tapes. Occasionally the electromagnetic energy field is precipitated causing the illusion of a ghostly apparition or an eerie cacophony of disembodied sounds. However, these are simply recordings somehow 'locked' in what is sometimes called the 'Stone Tape' phenomenon, eerie manifestations of a so-called 'haunted house'.

Thought Forms are in fact created through the same process, and by focusing the attention on something for any length of time, one is able to mentally create and release an incredibly powerful force. In all cases, the mind is the common denominator, and a powerful entity the potential of which is still as yet to be fully realised. If, as they say, 'the mind can put you into an early grave,' then through the same process, it can also heal and increase one's longevity.

CHAPTER SEVEN

THE MIND AND SELF-HEALING

As a child I was plagued with poor health, and as a consequence spent many weeks of the year in hospital having some sort of treatment or other. As a result of whooping cough I had developed Bronchiectasis, a serious lung disease for which there was no cure. Obviously in the mid to late fifties antibiotics were more or less in their innovative stages, and so the prognosis for my condition was quite clear – my parents were told in no uncertain terms that I would not live to see my tenth birthday. This meant that I was mollycoddled and prevented from getting involved in the recreational activities of other children. I suppose that as a result of spending many hours by myself I became quite introverted and very insecure. Although the word 'death' was always around me, and my future always spoken of in hushed tones, I never really believed that I was going to die. I had been psychically and mediumistically inclined ever since I can remember, and so I had always been in touch, so to speak, with the *Spirit World*, and 'seeing' so-called 'dead' people for me was common place. The problem was, I believed that everyone could see what I could see. Of course, this was simply not the case. So, I suppose one could say that I was an extremely unusual child, and to some, quite odd!

Although I had studied and practised meditation in the sixties (it was quite fashionable to do so then) my interest in metaphysics really only developed around 1970 when it was made clear to me that I had a vocation. By then I had learned to control and live with my lung condition, and I found that my practise of yoga and a certain method of meditation really was one of the primary reasons that my health condition no longer prevented me from leading a fairly normal life. I had spent so long living under the dark cloud of death that I frequently went into long periods of depression. Meditation and yoga helped me greatly, but it wasn't until I met Desmond Tierney, a teacher by profession, that my life really changed. Desmond Tierney was a spiritual healer with an interest in all things metaphysical. He had been trained by Alexander Cannon, a psychiatrist and well-known occultist. Des Tierney was a mine of information and seemed to always have the answers to my never-ending questions. In fact, he introduced me to the right books, the right courses, and the right way. As well as giving me Spiritual healing three and sometimes four times a week, he taught me how to control my thoughts, and how to use meditation as a means of healing myself. Needless to say, as soon as he could see that I was ready, Desmond Tierney walked out of my life as quickly as he had walked into, leaving me with a wealth of knowledge but with many, many still unanswered questions. One of the most important things I learnt from Desmond Tierney was that it is never too late neither to change nor to learn. I had spent a lifetime creating an emotional mess, and I was now faced with the process of psychologically reprogramming my mind. This was not going to be easy and I knew only too well what an arduous task lay ahead of me.

I had spent the period between 1962 up unto 1970 playing lead guitar in a rock band touring and living in various European countries. This was really all I had ever wanted to do and could not imagine doing anything else. As far as I had always been concerned, being psychic was not something I had to do. Besides, in those days nobody ever made a living from psychic or mediu-mistic abilities (unlike today) and the world of Rock music was far more exciting. My downfall really came when I began exper-imenting with chemical substances. At first I was only using amphetamines to stay awake. Cocaine and acid (Lysergic Acid) were fashionable, and as long as you indulged like everyone else, you fitted in perfectly. Unfortunately for me I had an extremely addictive personality and so I did not stop there! By 1970 my life was a veritable wreck and my musical career non-existent. I was so ill I returned from France to the UK to be nursed by my mother.

I now had to do something, and do something very fast. Desmond Tierney set the wheels in motion and I began working on myself.

One of the first things I had to learn was to relax. I had sustained a great deal of emotional and psychological damage during my years of drug abuse. Relaxing was extremely difficult and so that was first on my psychological programming agenda.

MY RELAXATION METHOD

The majority of those suffering from tension and anxiety find it difficult to accept that they are in actual fact suffering from these debilitating modern age conditions. So, to prove to yourself just how tense you really are, this is what to do:

- *Lie on the bed with your arms by your side. Breathe in and out for a few moments, ensuring that the inhalations and exhalations are evenly spaced.*
- *Now, make fists and clench your teeth and screw-up your face, and make your body as rigid as you possibly can. In fact make your whole body as tense as possible, ensuring that the muscles in your legs, tummy, buttocks and spine are so tight that your whole body trembles with the tension. Maintain this tensing process for a few moments, until you can no longer carry it on.*
- *Now, relax as completely as you possibly can – let go. Mentally scan your whole body making certain that all the nerves, muscles, tissues and fibres are relaxed. Relax all the muscles in your face, your forehead and around your eyes. Relax your chest and your stomach, your legs, your arms, hands and even your feet.*

- Sink into the bed and feel that overwhelming sense of calm washing all over you. Remain in this state for at least ten minutes.

- Conclude the exercise with some rhythmic breathing. Slowly breathe-in (allowing your tummy to rise,) breathe out (allowing your tummy to fall) and so on. Maintain a slow and easy rhythm, allowing yourself to sink deeper and deeper into relaxation.

- Now, as you breathe-in, mentally say to yourself, 'I breathe-in', and when you breathe-out, say to yourself, 'I breathe-out', and so on.

- Follow this as you breathe-in by mentally saying to yourself, 'relaxed,' and as you breathe-out, say to yourself, 'calm.' In fact, make these two words your personal mantras to be used every time you practise your relaxation routine. RELAXED AND CALM. Maintain this for a further few minutes and then relax.

Tensing your body in this way allows you to see exactly how tension makes you feel. It is exhausting and drains all your energy reserves. If you allow tension to persist, in the long-term it will cause all types of illness. Taking yourself through a daily routine of relaxation establishes feelings of peace and calm in the subconscious mind, and this will gradually filter through into the conscious mind producing an overwhelming effect upon your whole life.

RELAXATION AND SELF-HEALING METHOD I

It lies within your power to draw large reinforcements of energy from outside. The mind is an incredible computerised system containing a million components of energy just waiting to be activated. Once we have learned to access this computerised system you will then be capable of achieving anything and nothing whatsoever will be beyond your reach. One of the oldest Gnostic precepts is 'Man know thyself'. I would like to add to this,

'Believe in yourself and know that nothing is impossible!' A person who possesses low esteem and lacks motivation and drive has probably taken a lifetime to be like that. It's true to say that one can have a genetic predisposition to these psychological and emotional inadequacies, but generally speaking circumstances make the majority of people who and what they are. As a child we are programmed and conditioned to some extent by our parents, and the kind of young adults we eventually become is mostly as a consequence of that parental conditioning. Unless we possess sufficient inherent intelligence and awareness of ourselves, with the motivation to break free, we are then forced to face living the life that our parents have imposed upon us. It may well be that you are happy with that life, but the majority aspire to greater things and constantly endeavour to achieve success, wealth and happiness.

The mind has the power to achieve anything and nothing is beyond its reach. The majority of people have little or no under-standing of the metaphysical powers of the mind, and any hopes and dreams they may harbour forever remain just hopes and dreams. As a child my parents instilled in me that I was sickly and would never lead a 'normal' life. As I trusted my parents I had no reason to doubt what they were saying. Although I had a happy childhood and loving parents, they had no idea the immense burden they placed upon my shoulders. It wasn't until I was 14 years of age that something deep within me came 'alive'. I knew then that I had to think outside the parameters of my parents' range of thinking, and before I could even hope to repro-gramme my mind I had to de-clutter what they had taken 14 years to instil in me. I'm not suggesting for one moment that I just sat down and accomplished this in a couple of weeks; on the contrary, it was a slow and very difficult process, and one with which I am still faced today. I am quite sure that the majority of people are just like me, and perhaps only a small minority are quite happy to continue with the lives their parents created in them. Nonetheless, the self healing process is extremely effective, but must be applied on different levels.

MUSIC AS A THERAPY

Research into the effects of music on the human psyche has revealed that as humans evolved, music was intricately woven into the lives of virtually every culture around the world. It is a proven scientific fact that music is a part of our biological makeup, and is encoded in our genes as an integral part of what makes us human. It has been shown that listening to relaxing music produces theta brainwaves that are similar to those in deep relaxation and stage 1 of sleep. Music in fact holds our attention and distracts our thoughts away from worries, anxieties and concerns. Music is very often a repetitive mental stimulus that provides constant input into the sensory receptors of the brain, lowering arousals and inducing relaxation. More astoundingly, music can even evoke ancient memories within our DNA encouraging the pleasure and excitement experienced by our ancestors to surface in our consciousness. Music should then be an integral part of the self-healing process, which will help to encourage the release of endorphins in the brain promoting calmness and serenity.

Very little skill is required to administer metaphysical healing to one's self, and once the technique has been learned and fully understood, very little effort will be required. We explained in an earlier chapter about the structure and nature of the chakras and how they control, modify and distribute energy throughout the subtle anatomy, maintaining balance and harmony in the body. When we are out of sorts the individual chakras malfunction, causing the process of energy distribution to break down. Although the chakras eventually recover by themselves, their rate of recovery is extremely slow, and even then the chakra system as a whole is usually out of sync and therefore not efficient.

Let us take a look at one of many extremely effective self-healing methods.

- *For this you will need to sit on a straight back chair preferably in the garden (weather permitting) or facing an open window.*
- *Play some soothing meditative music in the background, and burn some pleasant incense.*
- *As previously suggested, sit with your chest, neck and head as nearly in a straight line as possible, eyes closed and hands resting lightly on your lap.*
- *Spend five or ten minutes breathing rhythmically until the rhythm is fully established in your mind.*
- *Now, allow your mind to drift from your breathing until you become completely unconscious of it, but at the same time still maintaining an evenly spaced rhythm.*
- *Mentally breathe in through the top of your head, watching the breath follow a vertical route between your brows, to your throat and then via your heart and naval, all the way down to the coccyx at the very base of your spine.*
- *Hold the breath, and on the exhalation mentally see the outpouring breath vertically ascend, following the same route back straight through the top of the head.*
- *Repeat the same process for ten minutes, longer if you feel you can, and then relax for a few moments, still with your eyes closed.*

Relaxation self-healing method 2

- *Still sitting with your eyes closed, allow your arms to fall to your sides (so that they hang loosely), and as you breathe in slowly raise your arms up into a horizontal position; hold your breath for a count of three, and then as you exhale slowly draw-in your arms until the palms of your hands are flat against your chest.*
- *Still with your hands flat against your chest, hold your breath for*

the count of three, and then breathe-in slowly, and when the breath is complete, whilst holding it again for the count of three, slap your chest forcibly with both hands, before releasing the breath in a long exhalation allowing your hands to fall to your sides on the conclusion.

- *Repeat the whole process no more than two times, and then relax with your eyes closed.*

This exercise facilitates the flow of prana in the lungs and encourages the movement of bio-electrical energy around the body. It is effective when there is a chest infection or when you are recovering from flu. Should you overdo the exercise it may cause feelings of disorientation and breathlessness. However, these feelings will pass within moments. On the conclusion of the exercise consume a glass of water to hydrate the body.

When embarking upon the path of healing, the following ancient precept should be borne in mind, 'Physician heal thyself'.

CHAPTER EIGHT

FINE TUNING THE BODY

We have already discussed the function of the chakra system and the part it plays in the manifestation of consciousness; but it is a little known fact that the individual chakras also resonate to specific musical notes, and when these are even slightly out of tune the whole body suffers as a consequence. Although this concept is not generally accepted as a common fact, it is nonetheless one that has been used through antiquity in many cultures. I refer to this anatomical system as *'Fine Tuning the Body'*, as the individual components of which the body is comprised collectively create a musical sound, in fact the *'Key of Life'*.

I have explained in a previous chapter that recent scientific studies into the way in which the human psyche is affected by music has shown conclusively that music is somehow integrated into our biological makeup and that our genetic structure is actually encoded with music, making us who and what we are. In fact, even though we humans have taken millions of years to evolve into the sentient, self-aware beings we are today, music has always been there, tightly woven into virtually every culture across the planet.

Not only does music have a profound effect upon the brain, it also has a significant *'washing'* effect on the bioluminescence of the aura, thus making it more stabilised and together. The effects of music on the body are in fact holistic and are like an incredible healing balm, encouraging both the body and mind to recover from illness. In fact, music produces long-term effects on the bioluminescence of the aura, and studies have shown that music can heal a broken or fragmented aura and even encourage a more consistent flow of energy and colour to the overall bioluminescence.

If you perceive the whole human form as a sequence of musical sounds, then you may be able to appreciate the concept of 'Fine Tuning' as I call it, and then be able to see that the body itself is rather like a musical instrument and will occasionally go completely out of tune.

Some people have the unusual skill of being able to 'listen' to their own body and to know exactly when it is even slightly off key. Such people are quite fortunate and nearly always enjoy good health. As just stated, the individual components that comprise the whole body mass collectively culminate into an incredible sound, usually inaudible to the ear, but discernable with the help of some basic tuning instruments (explained later) which are used to amplifier the various tones of the body. The overall sound of the body is the individual's so-called *Key of Life*, and is a combination of various notes created at different points and levels in the body. Should one of these notes be slightly off key, then the overall sound will appear slightly out of tune, just like listening to someone singing who is tone deaf. When the body is perfectly in tune, it has a resonance and is in perfect harmony with everything and everyone else. This means that the body, mind and spirit are balanced too and that the equilibrium is perfectly synchronised. To explain this phenomenon I always use the analogy of two guitars placed in opposite corners of a room; when a string is plucked on one of the guitars, the corresponding string on the other guitar resonates in sympathy. This illustrates the phenomenon of *Harmony* perfectly well I think, and also explains how we affect everything and everyone around us when we ourselves are finely tuned!

Although we have previously discussed the major chakras and their function as transformer-like units, modifying the volume and intensity of inflowing energy, we now need to turn our attention to the musical value of each of the seven major chakras. Each chakra emits a note, and each note vibrates to a particular colour, from the lowest on the visible spectrum (red) to the highest (violet/purple):

CHAKRA:	NOTE	COLOUR
1st *(Base)*	*C*	*RED*
2nd *(Splenic)*	*D*	*ORANGE*
3rd *(Solar plexus)*	*E*	*YELLOW*
4th *(Heart)*	*F*	*GREEN*
5th *(Throat)*	*G*	*BLUE*
6th *(Brow)*	*A*	*INDIGO*
7th *(Crown)*	*B*	*VIOLET/PURPLE*

Although the chakra system is potentially the same in everybody, in the majority of people one particular chakra tends to predominate. The sound of this chakra is generally therefore an indication as to the person's Key of Life, and as a consequence of stress, worry, poor diet and general wrong living its sound may either sharpen or flatten. This is not too detrimental to an individual's overall balance if the chakra's key only sharpens or flattens a semitone, but when it is subjected to *over tuning* perhaps as a result of living life in the fast lane, so to speak, the chakra's pitch moves a full tone and so changes key completely. When this change of key takes place it becomes more difficult to normalise the chakra again. This not only causes the individual to become highly stressed and oversensitive but, just like the analogy of the two guitars, the individual's surrounding environment is greatly affected as a consequence. This is the Law of Attraction in operation; we affect everything and everyone simply by *being*.

The most sensitive and spiritual individuals are those who live in the third chakra around the solar plexus and the seventh chakra on the crown of the head. In music the sounds of these chakras do not, technically speaking, have sharps. The third chakra resonates to the note of E, which when it sharpens becomes F, and the seventh chakra resonates to the note of B, which when it sharpens becomes C. Highly spiritually developed individuals, such as those who devote their lives to prayer, meditation and helping those in need, usually live out their lives in the Crown Chakra (Sahasrara) and the resonating sound of B. Although Crown Chakra people do not normally live in the real world, they are usually together and well balanced, and so their other chakras are usually tuned and well aligned.

Although aligning and tuning the chakras will not solve all the problems that may have turned your life upside down, the process will enable you to perceive things in a much more positive and philosophical way.

DETERMINING YOUR KEY OF LIFE

There are various more complicated ways of determining your key of life but I always find the most effective way is also the simplest.

For this process you should ideally have a full octave of tuning forks or similar tuning instruments, seven metal discs (approximately one inch in diameter,) a pendulum and the help of a friend on whom to experiment.

Part I of the experiment:

- *Lie the patient or friend in a horizontal position, preferably on the floor with a pillow to support his or her head.*
- *Place the seven metal discs more or less where the chakras are located strategically along the body, following a straight route, from the forehead to the genital area. Although the crown chakra is included in the whole process, in the majority of people the energy at this point is either inconsistent or exhibits a dormant or non-active polarity. Primarily for this reason the polarity of the chakras in this experiment is only monitored from the brow*

chakra. Because it would not be possible to place a disc on the exact location of the Crown Centre, you should place it as far back on the forehead as possible, with the brow centre disc exactly between the brows.

- *First of all, to ascertain the polarity of each chakra, they should be dowsed in sequential order, beginning with the chakra between the brows, and then following a straight route to the chakra at the base of the spine. Once a clockwise or anticlockwise motion has been established, move along to the next chakra and so on.*

- *Ideally, the movement of each chakra in a male should alternate from clockwise to anticlockwise, and the chakras of a female should rotate the opposite way. For example, the brow chakra of a male should rotate with a clockwise motion, and then the throat chakra with an anticlockwise motion, and so on, and the brow chakra of a female should exhibit an anticlockwise motion, and so on.*

- *Once all the chakras have been successfully dowsed, and their individual movements established and noted on a pad, the process of determining the person's 'Key of Life' can then commence.*

Part two of the experiment:

- *Strike the tuning fork of B and hold the end of it against the metal disk on the Crown chakra. Whilst holding it with one hand, hold the pendulum directly over it with the other, noting any change in the polarity. As I have already said this point may either be non active or exhibit inconsistent movements. Nonetheless, you should find that the tuning fork will produce some sort of change in the activity of this chakra.*

- *Next, strike the A tuning fork and place this on the metal disc between the brows, holding the pendulum directly over it. Again, make a note of any significant changes in the overall polarity.*

- *Place the G tuning fork against the metal disc on the throat area and dowse this as before, again making a note of any change in the movement of the pendulum.*
- *Following the same procedure as with the other chakras, strike the F tuning fork and place this against the metal disc in the location of the heart centre.*
- *Strike the E tuning fork and place this against the metal disc on the solar plexus centre, and dowse this.*
- *The D tuning fork should be then struck and placed against the metal disc in the area of the Splenic chakra and then dowsed.*
- *Finally, strike the C tuning fork and place this against the metal disc in the genital area, and then dowse it, again making a note of any noticeable changes in activity.*

Now, examine the results of the process to determine the person's Key of Life, paying particular attention to the notes of E and B.

The chakra displaying the most consistent movement is the one that should give you the overall Key. However, once you have established that this is the predominant chakra, it should be checked further to ensure that the results have been accurate and not misread. The rotation of the chakra that has seemingly produced the most consistent activity should now move in the opposite direction to its initial one. Occasionally the chakra giving you the Key of Life may already rotate the opposite way to all the other chakras, but will appear to become agitated once the appropriate note has been sounded.

To make certain that a correct reading has been obtained, results should be checked a couple of times, and a further couple of times the following day.

Although quite an arduous process, it is quite worth the effort, as knowing a person's Key of Life is extremely helpful in many areas of the individual's life. For example, listening to music that it perfectly synchronised with the listener has an incredible holistic effect upon the individual. Also, ascertaining a person's Key of Life can help a healer to determine a great deal about an individual's psychological and emotional well-being.

When an individual is suffering from a lot of minor health conditions and never seems to be psychologically or emotionally right, this may well be as a consequence of a significant change in the tonal effects of the individual's chakra notes, and his or her Key of Life may have made a dramatic change into a completely different key. I explained earlier that those with the Key of Life of either E or B are usually very sensitive and extremely creative and nearly always psychically inclined. When E changes a semi-tone it becomes F, and when B changes a semi- tone it becomes C, changing his or her personality and temperaments completely.

THE DIFFICULTY IN THE ASSESSMENT

The difficulty of course is actually ascertaining whether the Key of E and B are the original Keys or whether they have undergone a change. The consistency of the results accompanied by your intuitive skills as a healer should tell you this. As a healer you should always be guided by instinct and always go with your first feelings.

The tonal effects of the individual chakras can be maintained by relaxation, frequent healing applications and meditation.

FINAL COMMENT:

Should you have difficulty in obtaining tuning forks, a piano or guitar will suffice. Although not as effective, simply by asking someone to sound the appropriate notes in a continuous, consistent way, whilst you dowse the chakras will produce results. However, done in this way results will need to be checked several times to confirm they are correct.

CHAPTER NINE

SUGGESTIVE HEALING

In the same way that placebo medication will very often produce remarkable results on a person where there is suspicion of a psychosomatic condition; the same approach in an oral sense can also produce positive results on a condition, whether psychosomatic or otherwise. However, *Suggestive Healing* can only be successfully achieved when the practitioner fully understands the fundamental principles of *suggestion*, and is able to transmit streams of his or her own *bioelectrical* vitality with the oral suggestion. As discussed in a previous chapter, Franz Anton Mesmer was a practitioner of this method of healing, and although his innovative treatment of so-called 'Mesmerism' quickly caught on and was practised fairly successfully by many of his devotees, Mesmer himself knew quite well that such treatment would not work effectively unless the practitioner was able to draw-in and retain large stores of biomagnetism in his or her system. We have already explored the phenomenon of how some individuals naturally retain large amounts of prana in their bodies, and that when we are out of sorts, in their presence we feel 'full of beans' – in fact, full of their beans.

Once you fully understand this phenomenon and the concept of 'controlled transmission of bioelectrical vitality', then you can begin the oral treatment of suggestion. However, at this point it must be said that not all people are susceptible to suggestion, particularly when they are in the possession of a strong *will* and character. Even when they are willing participants in the healing process, such people take great pains to resist suggestion given either through hypnosis or subliminal messages. However, patience, persistence and determination nearly always bring about successful results.

Suggestive Healing is based upon the effect of mental influence over another person's subconscious mind. In much the same that an adverse suggestion can very easily produce abnormal conditions in an individual's body, so can a good suggestion help to restore normal conditions by encouraging recovery from illness. In fact, Suggestive Healing has on occasions successfully been used to encourage a seriously ill person to recover, just as if the patient had been suffering from a psychologically induced condition. In fact, the axiom of Suggestive Therapeutics is *'Thought takes form in Action'* and *'As a Man Thinketh in his heart, so is he.'*

Any method used to relieve or eradicate fear would most certainly cure disease. It makes sense then that the way to produce either a positive or negative effect on an individual's body is to infiltrate his or her mind.

Physicist, Sir George Paget Thomson, Nobel Prize winner for physics in 1937 was reported as saying, *'In many cases I have seen reasons for believing that cancer has its origins in prolonged anxiety.'*

Sir Benjamin Ward Richardson M.D who made many lucid contributions to popular medical literature, and also gave many inspired lectures on scientific subjects in the nineteenth century was also noted as saying, *'Eruptions on the skin will follow excessive mental strain. In all of these and in cancer, epilepsy and mania from mental causes there is a predisposition. It is remarkable how little the question of physical disease from mental influences has been studied.'*

Professor Elmer Gates, noted psychologist and lecturer conducted a great deal of research on the subject of the mind and how it can be easily influenced. During his scientific career he evolved a practical system of brain or mind building by systematic means, which causes an increase in the structural elements of brain cells, fibres and whole nervous system, and encourages an increase in mental capacity and skill. Professor Gates also made numerous other discoveries in experimental psychology out of which he evolved a method of using the mind more efficiently in the processes of discovery, invention, education and right living. In the late nineteenth century, the notable professor was recorded as saying: *'My experiments show that irascible, malevolent and depressing emotions generate in the system injurious compounds, some of which are extremely poisonous; also that agreeable, happy emotions generate chemical compounds of nutritious value, which stimulate the cells to manufacture energy.'*

In the latter part of the nineteenth century, British Psychiatrist, Professor Daniel Hack Tuke gives many examples in his book, *The Influence of the Mind upon the Body*, where the mind has exerted great power over disease caused by fear, worry or fright, the principal ones being as follows: insanity, idiocy, paralysis of various muscles and organs, profuse perspiration, jaundice, turning the hair grey, baldness, decay of the teeth, nervous shock followed by fatal anaemia, uterine troubles, skin diseases eczema etc. He also remarks upon the effect of fear in the spread of disease, particularly contagious diseases. Cholera epidemics are believed to have been largely due to the fear of the people in former times.

If, as the saying goes, we can worry ourselves into an early grave, then it makes sense then that we can also think ourselves into a healthier, happier and longer life. The principles cannot apply to one and not the other. The mind is in fact the common denominator, and it has the power to destroy and the incredible power to heal.

The practitioner of Suggestive Healing has the task of restoring normal mental conditions in someone who has probably spent a lifetime habitually thinking abnormally about their body. In fact, the practitioner has the responsibility of orally encouraging an abnormal *thinker* to believe that he or she is well or has the power to make themselves well. In some cases it is necessary for the practitioner of Suggestive Healing to instil in the patient a 'lie' by means of a 'loaded' sequence of words, thereby reprogramming the patient's mind to think in a different way. If a room full of twenty people tell one person that the decor is blue when it is in fact red, that one person will eventually begin to doubt what they are seeing. Although that example is a bit extreme it is in fact one of the fundamental principles underlying Suggestive Healing. Of course, there would always be one individual who would dismiss what the twenty people are saying as 'ridiculous'. As I have already stated some people are not susceptible to 'suggestion' and are therefore not receptive in any way whatsoever. Suggestive Healing should not be confused with so-called 'Mental Healing', a method that works purely by the process of *Thought Transference* and which can be conducted at a great distance. We have given an example of Mental Healing in a previous chapter and you will see from what I have said there that no verbal suggestion is required with that method, unlike Suggestive Healing which is dependent on it. It should also be borne in mind that Suggestive Healing is not Hypnosis, which is a specific therapy. For one thing, with Suggestive Healing there is no need to place the patient in a hypnotic state before the *suggestions* are made, and he or she is in total control of their faculties. Researchers exploring the effect of Suggestions on the mind of a patient concluded that they are just as effective as those made during a hypnotic treatment.

Before attempting the Suggestive treatment it should be borne in mind that the results are solely dependent on the receptivity of the individual. Although it is not absolutely essential for the patient to have prior knowledge of what the healer is doing, even a little cooperation will help the effectiveness of the treatment.

PREPARATION:

- *Before beginning the Suggestive Treatment the healer should ensure that the patient is receptive and is in a relaxed frame of mind.*

- *A confident healing practitioner should have very little difficulty bringing about a state of receptivity, and the patient's confidence should easily be secured by talking softly to them in reassuring tones.*
- *The healer should always pay great attention to his voice and should take care to speak with feeling and sincerity.*
- *Make every endeavour to cultivate a determined yet relaxing tone, and make certain that 'power' is imparted with your words.*
- *When speaking to the patient make certain that you look him or her in the eyes at all times. Allowing your gaze to wander from theirs during the dialogue is an indication of insincerity, and would merely defeat the object of the whole exercise.*
- *It is important for the healer to believe totally in what he or she is saying, as only then will the sentiment of what is being said be transferred directly to the patient's subconscious mind.*

THE SUGGESTIVE TREATMENT:

- *Suggestive healing should be given in a peaceful environment where you know the patient will not in any way be distracted.*
- *When a patient has no confidence or self-esteem, the healer should convince them otherwise by implanting the idea in their mind that he or she is 'exceptionally amazing'. Key words should be interjected into the dialogue, such as 'AMAZING', with emphasis on the word. Confidence building is an integral part of the whole process.*
- *When an individual is suffering from a physical illness, whether serious or otherwise, the healer should firmly instil in the patient that they are going to get well, sooner rather than later. When the outlook appears hopeless for the patient, the healer should make every attempt to convince them otherwise.*
- *Suggestive Healing involves reversing the mental attitude of the patient, encouraging in them the belief that they ARE going to*

get well.

- *Before attempting Suggestive Healing the dialogue should first be created, and if necessary learnt by rote to ensure it is orally given with confidence and determination.*
- *The whole process of Suggestive Healing is dependent on the transmission of the dialogue and also the power of accompanying biomagnetism – that is the healer's personal charismatic energy.*
- *Because of the intensity of the Suggestive Healing process, the healer usually feels drained after the treatment. It is important to see only one patient a day so as not to deplete your own energy levels. Most illnesses, particularly psychological disorders, are very often contagious and precautions should always be taken not to overdo it.*
- *During the Suggestive Healing Treatment it is important to be consistent in your choice of dialogue with repetition of all 'Key' words to obtain maximum results.*
- *The practitioner should also use the same dialogue in different ways so as to subliminally 'fix' the suggestion firmly in the patient's mind. Always let the 'Key' word be emphasised thus catching the patient unawares. In this way will the suggestion be lodged so to speak in his or her mind.*

When taking a patient through Suggestive Healing Treatment it is important not to make any direct reference to their health condition, but always divert his or her attention away from it by suggesting to them how their health is going to be. The healer should actually 'see' in his or her mind's eye what they are endeavouring to achieve with the Suggestive Treatment. In other words the healer should always have a mental picture of the conditions he wishes to bring about. In order to achieve positive results it is sometimes necessary to implant a so-called 'placebo lie' in the patient's subconscious mind, thus making them truly believe that recovery is more than a possibility. Occasionally this approach can bring about remarkable results, even though the healer may secretly feel that he has 'tricked' the patient into recovery. The tactic is unimportant as long as recovery is achieved.

To many people the Suggestive Treatment method does not fit comfortably under the umbrella of 'healing'. Anything that brings about a cure on any level should always be regarded as 'Healing', as Suggestion is an integral part of any healing treatment.

CHAPTER TEN

SPIRITUAL HEALING

As far as I am concerned Spiritual Healing is highly specialised and a completely different phenomenon to other forms of healing. Just as mediums are born and not made, so too are Spiritual Healers born with the potential and most certainly not created. One can have a great desire to heal the sick, but unless the potential is present positive results will never be achieved. Many healers mistakenly believe that they are administering *Spiritual Healing* when they are not! True Spiritual Healing is extremely rare and involves a lot more than the simple process of the laying on of hands. I know that this may greatly offend many practitioners of Spiritual Healing who may probably dismiss the whole book on that statement. Nonetheless, this is my belief and is something I discovered the hard way, which I will explain later on in the chapter. In previous chapters we have explored some of the different areas of healing and I have explained about the fundamental principles of energy and exactly how a healer can exploit it for the purpose of transferring vitality to another person. The process of Pranic healing is primarily to do with the degree of prana drawn into and retained in the healer's body, whilst Spiritual Healing is connected in many ways to the healer's 'attunement' with higher and more refined *Spiritual Forces*. Unfortunately, good intentions is not enough to be a Spiritual Healer, as much more is required of the individual in the way of dedication, devotion, character and the development of Spiritual Consciousness. All this may sound almost super-spiritual and may even put a lot of potential healers off the whole process. Nonetheless, this is something that must be addressed before we move on into the realms of Spiritual Healing, the highest form of metaphysical treatments. Many people reading this book purely out of interest may unknowingly possess the potential to be a Spiritual Healer, and so it is hoped that by the end of the book I will have helped them to realise their true potential.

You may well ask 'How do I know which method of healing I am to use?' The primary object of this book is to stimulate the interest initially so that you will be sufficiently motivated to explore all areas of metaphysical healing. It may well be that you do have the potential to be a Spiritual Healer, but initially it would be a good idea to explore all aspects of healing.

Should you have no real interest in the mechanics of healing but simply have a strong desire to administer healing to the sick, this may be an indication that you do possess the inherent ability to be a spiritual healer.

Spiritual healing is a process of attunement during which the healer initially places his or her hands on the patient's shoulders. Although a very small part of the healing force manifests from the healer's own aura, most of the healing originates from an external spiritual source and upon entering the healer is transmuted and immediately directed to the affected part of the patient's anatomy. This means that the healer's hands do not have to be applied directly to the affected part of the body. The head is an extremely effective part of the body with which to begin the healing treatment.

When endeavouring to develop your spiritual healing potential a great deal of discipline is required and it is also necessary for the healer to apply himself to the study of the Spiritual Healing process. When practising any form of metaphysical healing it should always be borne in mind that it is unethical, and in some cases illegal to offer a diagnosis or suggest withdrawing prescribed medicine. The healer is merely the instrument through which a spiritual force flows into the patient. Although cures brought about through Spiritual Healing treatment can on rare occasions be instantaneous, it should be realised that some people can never be healed, especially if the condition with which they are suffering is a longstanding one and is therefore well and truly established in his or her subconscious mind. On rare occasions a healer will encounter a patient who will hold on to their illness, simply because without it they would lose all the interest and concern shown to them by family members and friends. As a healer and sensitive you will probably know this immediately. In such cases the healer needs to psychologically de-armour the patient, just like the process of slowly peeling the layers of an onion until you finally get right down to the centre or in the patient's case the spirit.

DOS AND DONT'S

DO: Pay attention to personal hygiene.

DO: Spend some time quietly contemplating the treatment before the patient arrives, thus establishing a mental connection with them.

DO: Exchange some pleasantries before the healing treatment begins. This helps to put them at ease and make them feel comfortable with you.

DO: Have appropriate background music. This creates the right mood.

DONT: Offer a diagnosis or contradict the professional medical treatment he or she is currently having.

DON'T: Begin the treatment without first explaining what you are going to do.

DON'T: Behave as though what you are going to do is mysterious and special. Should the person be of a nervous disposition this approach will only suffice in making them anxious and tense defeating the whole object of the treatment.

DON'T: Give healing when you have a cold or feel under the weather.

DON'T: Allow your personal feelings to be apparent during healing treatment.

DON'T: Administer healing to a member of the opposite sex

unaccompanied.

DON'T: *Give healing to anyone with a highly contagious disease.*

As a healer you are bound to a moral code of practise and must therefore treat what you are doing with the utmost respect. Should you not belong to a recognised healing federation, than you would be wise to take out personal liability insurance to safeguard yourself.

Remember, Spiritual Healing is the highest form of healing, and although no specific visualisation techniques are required, you may well find that your healing is more effective when you integrate this into the treatment. It is always a good idea not to eat before a healing session, but make sure that you drink plenty of water before and after the healing treatment. Once you have established a fairly good relationship with your patient, the healing treatment will be greatly helped if you spend a few minutes focusing your attention on them before they arrive. This strengthens the connection you have with your patient and facilitates the healing force before you actually make physical contact with them.

Your sensitivity may mean that there are times when you find it difficult to separate yourself emotionally from your patient, and if you are giving healing on a fairly regular basis, the psychological effects of this can be quite difficult to deal with. The following visualisation exercise helps to clear your aura of any dross that might have accumulated, and will also stabilise your emotions.

CLEARING THE AURIC COLOUR

- *Sit on a straight backed chair, feet firmly on the floor and your hands resting lightly on your lap.*
- *Close your eyes and breathe rhythmically until the rhythm is fully established, ensuring that the inhalations and exhalations*

are evenly spaced.

- *When you feel quite relaxed, mentally build a red curtain of energy in front of you, from the floor all the way up to the ceiling above your head.*

- *Feel the heat of the red energy against your skin and deep inside you. Hold it for a few moments, and then dissolve the curtain of red energy from your mind.*

- *Now, mentally build a curtain of intense blue energy in front of you. Feel the coolness of the blue energy against your skin. See the blue energy peppered with sparkling golden light. Take a few deep breaths and draw the blue energy with the golden sparkles of light into your body. Hold your breath for a few moments allowing the blue energy to circulate your entire body, and then slowly breathe it all out.*

- *Finally, build a curtain of golden energy in front of you. Allow the golden energy to envelope your body completely. Breathe in and out a few times, and then as you exhale dissolve the imagery completely from your mind.*

- *Sit quietly for a few moments before opening your eyes.*

Visualising the colours in this way produces a sweeping effect on the aura and psychologically stabilises its energy flow. Although technically Spiritual Healing does not affect the healing practitioner, over a period of time the colours in his or her aura can fade and become slightly fragmented, thus permitting 'psychic germs' to infiltrate it. The above exercise prevents that from happening and also helps to revitalise the individual colours and overall appearance of the bioluminescence of the aura. Any use of the image-making faculty produces an extremely positive effect on the bioluminescence of the aura, essential when administering healing on a regular basis.

Contrary to popular belief, healers who specialise in certain diseases leave themselves wide open to auric infiltration, and if the condition is allowed to persist for any length of time deterioration of the practitioner's health will occur. This might sound absurd to some practitioners of spiritual healing, but when you look at it logically you may come to understand exactly why. Contact with another individual's personal energy field on a regular basis involves actual infiltration into his or her subtle energies. In time this becomes quite contagious and will cause fragmentations in the practitioner's aura at strategic points. To avoid such adverse effects healing treatments should ideally be limited to three or four times a week.

CHAPTER ELEVEN

HEALING THROUGH THE CHAKRAS

As previously explained, there are seven major chakras that are considered primary and these are located at strategic points across the surface of the etheric tract in the spinal column. They are connected to the endocrine glands and nerve plexuses through an extensive system of channels called 'Nadis'. It is along these channels that prana flows continuously from the chakras to the organs of the physical body, maintaining health and balance on all levels. By affecting the polarity of the individual chakras it is possible to encourage the movement of energy through the subtle channels, thus facilitating the balancing process. Remember, we are dealing with subtle energies, not only in the physical body, but also in the subtle or bioplasmic body, therefore it is not necessary to actually make physical contact with the person.

Although the individual chakras in the female rotate the opposite way to those in a male, when actually applying the treatment this should not concern you. As I explained in an earlier chapter, Chakra means 'wheel' or 'circle', each one a vibratory whirlpool of colour, constantly distributing prana throughout the body. Therefore, when the following treatment is applied it helps to normalise and increase the movement of each chakra without any attention being paid to their polarity.

The process of affecting the movement of each chakra requires a little concentration, primarily to ensure that the movement of the hands is perfectly synchronised. Therefore, you may have to practise your coordination a few times before actually applying the treatment.

THE PROCESS OF HAND ROTATION

- *Lie the patient in a horizontal position with his or her hands by their sides, and ensuring easy access to the locations of the chakras.*

- *Beginning with the head; place your left hand (fingers outstretched) about an inch away from the forehead, and place your right hand on top of your left hand (without touching it), and then commence moving your left hand in a clockwise, circular motion, and your right hand in an anticlockwise circular motion.*

- *Continue in that position for a few moments, and then allowing the motion to be maintained, slowly move your hands to the throat area, then to the heart area, and so on, until all the chakras have been treated.*

- *Once you have reached the base chakra, repeat the treatment in reverse. When the forehead has been reached, continue the treatment once again in reverse, and when the base chakra has been reached, suspend the treatment.*

- *Ask the patient to now lie face down, giving you easy access to his or her back.*

- *Apply the same process from the back of the head, down to the base of the spine, ensuring that the rotating process is maintained with a steady motion all through the treatment.*

- *Once you have completed the treatment on the back of the patient for several minutes, apply the same process down each arm, then down each leg.*

- *Once this has been completed, allow your instinct to guide you over the whole body.*

This treatment is ideal for encouraging the movement of prana throughout the whole body, helping to maintain the equilibrium of body, mind and spirit.

It may take you some time to get the coordination right and to administer the treatment with some confidence. Even though the patient's eyes are closed, he or she will still be aware of the pleasant sensation of energy moving through the subtle channels. Apart from everything else, this particular treatment has an overwhelming stimulating effect upon the brain, encouraging feelings of euphoria and well-being. Frequent applications help to maintain balance on all levels of the individual's health.

As mentioned previously, one of the functions of chakras is to modulate, control and distribute the in-pouring energy, ensuring that balance is maintained throughout the whole body. Each individual chakra is responsible for man's consciousness at that corresponding level, and therefore regulates the individual's holistic development on all levels of cognitive awareness. Whilst the chakras evolve quite naturally through the person's aspirations and endeavours, they can be greatly influenced with the above exercise for the precipitation of consciousness. Frequent use of the above treatment can help the cultivation and ultimate development of the faculties, thus safely encouraging the release of any psychic potential. To encourage changes in the polarity of the individual's chakras and aura, the same treatment may be applied holding a metal magnet in each hand during the rotational process. With this treatment there is no necessity to involve any visualisation or mental imagery, as the rotating hands produce a powerful effect upon the subtle areas of the aura as well as the individual chakras. This may all sound quite ridiculous to the sceptically minded person, but I would suggest that it be tried before any judgements are made. As I have explained in previous treatments the use of metal magnets have an extremely powerful effect upon the subtle energies as well as on the physical body.

You can stimulate your own chakras through the mental imagery of visualisation. Although the process may be applied when treating another person, it is more effective on yourself. Visualisation somehow has an incredible effect upon the subtle anatomy, and will completely change the polarity of each individual chakra when practised on a regular basis. Once again you would be advised not to dismiss the exercise purely because of its simplicity.

CHAKRA VISUALISATION

For this exercise it is essential to sit on a straight backed chair, with your back as straight as possible, shoulders thrown slightly back, and your hands resting lightly on your lap.

- *Spend five minutes imagining radiations of intense blue energy emanating from your body. In fact, surrounding you completely.*
- *Once you have established this imagery in your mind, and feel confident that it is fully under your control, gradually change the colour from blue to pure white. Maintain this imagery for a little while longer, and then allow it to slowly dissolve.*
- *Now, mentally see a shaft of intense white light, spiralling down from above you, through the top of your head, touching each chakra in sequential order, and finally dissipating as the chakra at the base of the spine is reached.*
- *Allow a few moments to elapse before repeating the same process. Mentally see the spiralling white light descending, through the crown of your head, infusing each chakra until it finally dissipates upon reaching the chakra at the base of the spine.*

The exercise should be repeated at least five times, and then concluded with some slow, rhythmic breathing.

The mental imagery of the spiralling light has a remarkable effect upon the individual chakras, causing them to be vivified even more into coruscating whirlpools of colour and light. The mental effect of this process is also holistic, precipitating the movement of energy in the physical as well as the subtle anatomy. After the conclusion of the exercise it is a good idea to drink a glass of fresh spring water. As previously suggested, before drinking the water pour it from one glass to another, over and over again, until it almost comes alive.

CHAPTER TWELVE

THE PRINCIPLES OF SELF-SUGGESTION

It is a known scientific fact that the combination of two atoms of hydrogen, and one of oxygen results in water. Also, one atom of oxygen and one atom of carbon will produce carbon monoxide, an extremely poisonous gas. But, by adding another atom of oxygen carbon dioxide will result, a harmless gas. The principles of chemistry, physics and mathematics are exactly the same as the principles of thought and the subconscious mind. Whatever thoughts you store in your subconscious mind, will most definitely have a corresponding effect upon the universe and ultimately manifest in your life as a condition, experience and an event. Just like the various combinations of atoms in chemistry, a single thought can produce a spontaneous reaction in your life, transforming it completely. Watching the way you think is not an easy exercise, considering that you have most probably taken a lifetime to fill your subconscious mind with negative thoughts produced by habitual thinking. Changing the habits of a lifetime is not easy, but not impossible. Giving healing when you yourself are mentally out of sync is pretty much like playing a guitar and not having a clue how to tune it when it goes out of tune. Regardless of what method of healing you are interested in, the precept, *'Physician heal thyself,'* should always be borne in mind, and every effort should be taken to maintain the efficiency of your mind. A person's health is very often brought about by his or her self-suggestion. If an individual maintains a positive mental attitude of health, strength and vitality, then these will manifest accordingly. And if the mind is filled with thoughts of a depressing nature the physical body will likewise respond. It is a known medical fact that fear is one of the greatest causes of disease. The chemicals produced in the body by fear are like poison to the system, and its effects manifest holistically, causing a broad spectrum of health problems. When fear is eradicated, in many cases so too is disease. Positive affirmations may be introduced into the subconscious mind to change the way in which thoughts are processed in the brain. Overhauling the mechanism of the mind in this way encourages a more positive attitude and approach to life generally. There is far more truth than might be realised in the ancient aphorism, *'As a Man Thinketh in His Heart So Is He'*. In fact, the psychological implications of this cover a broad spectrum, and probably account for most if not all of human failings. If a positive phrase is repeatedly chanted, over and over again, without giving the content of it a single thought, the effect upon the subconscious mind is still the same as when you are mindful of what you are saying. In fact, you can learn a phrase by rote, or even read it without even thinking what you are saying, it really does not matter, it will still impact the subconscious mind with positive results. An effective way of reprogramming the subconscious mind is through the psychological process of *Hypnopaedia* (sleep learning.) For that process it is more effective to use a pillow speaker and a loop recording of what needs to be learned. A pillow speaker is flat and fits comfortably in your pillow. Although some research has shown that sleep learning is ineffective, some experiments have concluded that nine out of ten people have a greater capacity to absorb information when they are asleep as opposed to when they are awake. Although the Hypnopaedia method can be used for mentally absorbing all sorts of data, it is also an extremely effective way of treating phobias of all kinds. If you encounter some difficulty obtaining a pillow speaker, an ordinary cassette player situated at the side of your bed will suffice. The fundamental principles are the same as repeating a phrase over and over again, almost until your brain seems to buzz.

The primary object of reprogramming the subconscious mind

is to reorganise the thought processing mechanism and change the way you think about yourself and your life. For example, should you have difficulty with self-esteem, the primary aim is to *convince* the subconscious mind that you are confident and capable of achieving anything at all. The same principles may be applied when you seem not to be successful in life and you always seem to fail in your endeavours. I suppose this method of rearranging your thoughts could be described as a sort of placebo effect, as it involves the process of telling yourself that you are confident when you know you are not. Even though this sounds impossible, it is, nonetheless, a process that is extremely effective, and can work in a very short space of time. Although I could give an endless list of examples of 'affirmations' and 'suggestions', as you know your own weaknesses, you are far better creating your own. Self suggestion should ideally be approached as though you are speaking to another person. In this way is your subconscious mind more likely to pay attention so to speak, and therefore respond more effectively. The affirmations you 'feed' into your subconscious mind are also more effective if your mental commands are positive and forceful. You could begin the process of reprogramming for example in this way, 'I want you to take notice of exactly what I am saying, and now begin to transform my life!' This passage needs to be repeated three or four times, after which your chosen affirmation should be used. Once you have mastered the technique of using self-created affirmations in this way, with the sole intention of reprogramming the subconscious mind, you will then become the master of your own thoughts.

Let us explore some of the affirmations that can be used. One of the most popular and simplistic ones when you are depressed or feeling under the weather is, *'Every day, in every way, I am feeling better and better and better.'* When this phrase is repeated over and over again, it really does seem to have an incredible effect upon your whole body, making it tingle and your brain buzz. Another is the affirmation we discussed earlier, *'I am healthy, wealthy, happy, successful and wise.'* This affirmation involves the process of convincing the subconscious mind that you already possess wealth and success even when your dreams have not yet been realised. Just as many people can make themselves sick by improper self-suggestion, so may they restore their health through the process of positive suggestions given in the same way. Once the subconscious mind has been filled with positive thoughts and ideas, they will then gradually filter through into the conscious mind to become a reality in the thinker's life. This is a well established and extremely powerful psychological law. Remember the aphorism: *'Thoughts crystallise into habit, and habit solidifies into circumstances.'* You may think that this is easier said than done, but it really only takes a little determined application in order to transform the way in which your mind processes your thoughts. Another extremely effective affirmation and one that produces results in a very short time is, *'I am one of the most positive people in the world! I have a powerful mind and am capable of achieving anything I want.'* Recite this 10 times upon rising, and then a further 10 times before retiring for the night. If you are seriously considering embarking upon the path of healing, you really do need to be positive, dynamic and spontaneous. It is sometimes necessary to instil positive ideas into the mind of a psychologically or emotionally disturbed person using the placebo process of dialogue. In other words, you must learn to convey a positive suggestion to the patient – even when it is not true. The onus is on the healing practitioner to 'convince' the weak minded individual that he or she is mentally powerful and strong. Before you are able to achieve such psychological results, you must be sufficiently positive yourself. Another excellent way for creating an extremely powerful body and mind is in the following use of *power words.*

THE HEALING EFFECTS OF POWER WORDS AND CHANTING

As we have previously discussed mantras form the basis of certain methods of meditation. In the 1960s, physicist, the Maharishi Mahesh Yogi, was the innovator of a method of meditation he called Transcendental meditation, or TM as it became popularly known. This involved chanting a word that was personal to the meditator, and was said to relieve stress and heighten the spiritual consciousness. In fact, the concept of chanting has been used by many cultures for thousands of years and has always been an extremely effective way of precipitating the consciousness into transcendental states of awareness. When mantras are used specifically to maintain balance in the body and mind, certain sounds may be effectively used. Although these can take many forms, the ones I have always used produce remarkable results and have a particular resonance with the individual chakras and the corresponding parts of the physical anatomy. These can also be used to heighten one's awareness by stimulating the pituitary and pineal glands.

If need be the mantras can be easily modified to suit you. To begin with, as I have already said, each mantra affects its corresponding part of the anatomy, and when chanted in sequential order, the overall vibratory sound of the body is increased, thus producing a powerful resonance with the universal pulse.

PROCESS OF INCREASING THE VIBRATORY RATE OF THE BODY

- *MMEE - This produces an amazing effect upon the pituitary and pineal glands, and encourages an increase in the electromagnetic waves emanating from the pineal gland. To use the mantra, inhale a complete breath, and then chant the word until all the breath has been fully exhaled. Repeat the process four times before moving on to the next.*

- **EA** - *Ea should be sounded as in the word 'feather'. This mantra affects the throat area, and particularly affects the thyroid. As previously explained, inhale a complete breath, and then sound the word until all the breath has been fully expelled. Repeat this four times before moving on to the next sound.*
- **AAA** - *Aaa should be sounded like the word 'Grass', following the same procedure as previously shown. This particular mantra affects the upper respiratory area of the body.*
- **OU-O** - *Ou-o should be sounded as in the word, 'water', with the same procedure as given with the previous mantras. The vibrations with this sound affect the middle area of the chest.*
- **Ooo** - *Ooo should be sounded like the word 'Home', again with the same breathing procedure as previously shown. This word has a remarkable effect upon the lower part of the lungs, the heart, stomach and liver.*
- **EUR** - *Eur should be sounded as in the French word 'Fleur', and chanted in the same way as the previously given words. The vibratory sounds of this word affect the diaphragm and surrounding area.*
- **U-EE** – *U-ee should be sounded as in 'You-ee', and allowed to resonate until the breath has been fully expelled. The vibratory sounds of this word affect the gonads of the male and female reproductory system.*

As I have previously explained, for maximum results, each word should be chanted no more than four times in sequential order each session. Even though positive results will be achieved in a very short time, you should persist with the practice for at least a month, longer if you feel comfortable. The different sounds increase the vibratory rate of the subtle anatomy and encourage a greater frequency of the movement of the individual chakras – the vortices of energy that lie along the surface of the etheric tract in the spinal column. As I have previously explained, the chakra system's responsibility is to encourage balance and equilibrium of body, mind and spirit, thus ensuring that the health of the body is maintained. Although there are hundreds of minor chakras situated all over the subtle anatomy, there are in fact seven major chakras that are considered primary. These are connected to the endocrine glands and nerve plexuses through an extensive system of channels called nadis. Nadi means 'nerve' only at a more subtle level, and it is along these nadis that Prana (discussed elsewhere) is conveyed from the chakras to the organs of the body. This incessant process of conveying energy is essential for the maintenance of the health in the physical body, and so understandably when it ceases to run as efficiently the health of the body is impaired. The chanting of the above words encourages the stimulation of all the major glands in the body, thus ensuring that the health is maintained.

An excellent mantra for stimulating the heart as well as the corresponding chakra is, 'MMMMMM-PO-MMMMMM. As this mantra vibrates the heart area, it would be advisable to use this only once a day. In fact, if there is a history of weakness in this area, the practitioner should begin by strengthening the heart first of all with a much shorter version. MMM-PO-MMM, followed by PAAAAEEEEEEE, in one long breath. Remember not to strain or make it a labour as this merely defeats the whole object of the exercise. A little experimentation may well help you to find other more suitable mantras that stimulate the different organs of the body. If they produce more effective results then by all means use them. Combinations of mantras may be integrated into your daily programme. As long as they stimulate you and do not make you feel exhausted, then you can rest assured that they are working for you

CHAPTER THIRTEEN

HEALING POWER OF COLOUR
AND WATER

I have spoken in an earlier chapter at some length about prana, and explained that in the esoteric traditions of yoga this word is used to describe all energy in the universe. Prana is the subtle agent through which the life of the body is sustained. It can be found working through all forms of matter, and is in the air we breathe and the water we drink. Prana is the principle responsible for the integration of the cells into a whole, and is the fundamental principle of animation. When the physical organism begins to age, prana usually has difficulty circulating the body as efficiently; as a direct result the movement of our body is impaired, our skin loses its elasticity and wrinkles, and when prana withdraws completely, we die. After death, the body begins to decay and disintegrate. The individual atoms of which the physical body is composed then run amok, taking with them sufficient prana to enable them to form new combinations. The remaining prana returns to the universal reservoir to continue its relentless function of sustaining life on the planet. Yogi Masters have always fully understood this amazing phenomenon and have learned how to slow down the process of death by controlling the inflowing prana into their bodies. As I have already previously explained they do this with a system of breathing they call Pranayama, meaning the control of prana, combined with a frugal, healthy diet to sustain the body's vitality. I have also explained that water is a conduit of the vital force, and so the physical organism derives a great deal of benefit when it is well hydrated. Irrigation of the cells is essential for the maintenance of the body's efficiency, and by taking the water through a stimulating process before it is drunk, encourages the prana contained in it to come 'alive'. I have already explained in a previous chapter how water should be poured from one drinking vessel to another, backward and forward, several times before it is drunk. Having subjected the water to this simple process, it can then be energised with colour vibrations to be used in the treatment of specific health conditions. The ancient Egyptian physicians used colour to treat all sorts of maladies of both the body and the mind. They fully understood the concept of colour and the way it affected the human organism. Although Chrometherapy (healing with colour) is today considered an alternative method of healing, the ancient Egyptians regarded it as a new science, and viewed the human body as a rainbow, consisting of seven distinct colours of varying degrees. They would diagnose illness by making a detailed analysis of the colour composition of the body, ensuring the whole spectrum was perfectly synchronised. I have already explained that coloured gauze filters were secured across openings on the roof of the colour surgery, below which the patient would be seated to be bathed in the filtered rays of the sun. The colour treatment had an incredible harmonising effect on the individual, who would usually be invigorated at the conclusion of the therapeutic session. More recently, chrometherapy experiments were carried out at a psychiatric unit in California. A psychotic patient had all his medication withdrawn and was left until he became extremely agitated and totally incoherent. He was then placed in a room where everything including the lighting was pink. Within an hour the patient calmed down and became quite coherent, just as though he was still highly medicated. In the early part of the twentieth century, a doctor caring for patients suffering from consumption at a New York sanatorium made some startling observations. The bed of a patient suffering from advanced consumption was moved in front of a window on a beautiful autumnal morning. Within an hour the woman had colour in her cheeks and the haemoptysis (coughing blood) had ceased. Her remarkable recovery was brought to the attention of the other doctors who were totally baffled. The head doctor then realised that the woman had been bathed in the sun's rays filtering through the stained blue glass window. Further experiments were carried out on other patients with the same startling results. In the early part of the twentieth century, Edwin D Babbitt (1828-1905) resurrected alchemical theories of the healing properties of certain colours, leading him to write his bestselling book, *THE PRINCIPLES OF LIGHT AND COLOUR*. Faber Birren, the renowned industrial consultant on colour remarked, *'Colour may not be as directly therapeutic as men once believed, but as a psychic or psychological force in healing, it is certainly efficacious.'* Regardless of how colour affects the human organism, it most certainly does work. It may well have a psychological effect upon a patient, but when it is used to affect water this cannot be the case.

INFUSING WATER WITH COLOUR VIBRATIONS

The health of the body cannot be maintained without our daily intake of water. In fact, our bodies are made up of seventy percent water, and should the organism be deprived of sufficient water to sustain it, then the efficiency of its performance is greatly affected. Apart from this, the prana contained in water can be greatly influenced by infusing it with colour encouraged by the rays of the sun. As we have already explained in a previous chapter how this is done there is no need for me to reiterate the process of colour charging water with the use of filters, but it is vitality important that you do understand that water charging is extremely powerful and can produce startling results in a very short time. Although medical practitioners have suggested that treating a sick person with colour charged water is purely psychological, when animals respond to the same treatment this suggestion does not in anyway stand up.

Another way to use colour charged water in the treatment of

illness is to apply it to pieces of cotton or wool fabric in the corresponding colour, leave it to dry naturally, and then allow the patient to sleep over night with it wrapped around the chest. This method may sound like the treatment of a quack practitioner, but believe me it is extremely effective. How and why it works I have no idea, but all I can say is that it is extremely effective in the treatment of many illnesses, ranging from simple respiratory conditions, to the more serious inflammatory diseases. I am not suggesting that such treatments are a substitute for conventional, allopathic medicine, but they most certainly complement the more traditional and accepted treatments. It has also been found that the healing force is somehow facilitated when some heat is applied to the coloured fabric. In extremely painful conditions, such as arthritis or rheumatics, the treatment sometimes becomes more powerful when red charged water is applied to blue cloth. Red and blue are extremely powerful and very often anaesthetise the body to pain.

THE EFFECTS OF COLOUR

- **RED:** *As well as physically warming the body, the psychological effects of red are extremely powerful. Red is effective in the treatment of blood conditions, and also when the patient is suffering from a low temperature. The combination of blue and red is extremely effective when the patient is lethargic and lacks energy and drive.*
- **ORANGE:** *This is an extremely effective colour in the treatment of dermatological conditions, especially when they result from a vitamin deficiency.*
- **YELLOW:** *The stimulating effects of yellow are effective in the treatment of Gaul bladder and kidney problems, and may also be used in the treatment of acute constipation. Combined with green, yellow is also effective in the treatment conditions affecting the endocrine glands.*

- **GREEN:** *Green being the colour of nature is also the colour of harmony and balance. In fact, although green is the traditionally accepted colour of the heart chakra, and therefore effective in the treatment of heart conditions, its harmonious vibrations have a holistic effect upon the human organism, thus encouraging equilibrium of body, mind and spirit. Its strength may be increased when combined with other colours.*
- **BLUE:** *The soothing rays of blue will reduce a high temperature and are also effective in the treatment of nervous or psychological disorders. Combined with purple, blue has an anaesthetising effect upon pain and will calm taut nerves.*
- **INDIGO:** *The healing properties of this colour cover a broad spectrum of ailments, from stomach and pancreatic conditions, to migraine and tumours. The power of indigo is greatly increased when combined with blue or purple.*
- **VIOLET:** *The most powerful colour on the visible spectrum, violet or purple may be used to treat all maladies of both the body and the mind, and will also increase the intensity and power of any other colour combined with it.*

Once the water has been charged it should be subjected to the pouring process for five minutes before it is drunk. Colour charged water can also be kept in a corresponding coloured bottle and stored in the refrigerator to be drunk when needed. Always pour it from one vessel to another, over and over again, for around five to eight minutes before it is consumed.

THE MUSICAL RAINBOW MAN

When using any form of colour therapy to treat illness, the body should be regarded as a unit of incredible power, divided into sections, each one in a colour of the spectrum. This approach should not be confused with the treatment covered in an earlier chapter on the Key of Life, and even though I refer to the chakras later, the process is given as an alternative method. The lower portion of the body is red, ascending in a vibratory scale, up to the head, which is violet. For the purpose of tuning, each coloured portion of the body, again beginning with red at the lowest section, corresponds with a different musical tone, as I explained in the chapter covering the musical tones of the chakras and the Key of Life. However, in this treatment we look at the whole body being divided into musical notes, as opposed to just the chakras. When we do this it becomes far easier to make a detailed analysis of the affected parts of the body when considering the treatment of individual diseases and the overall health of the person. Beginning with Red which, as we already know, has the musical tone of C, Orange vibrates to D, Yellow vibrates to E, Green vibrates to F, Blue vibrates to G, Indigo vibrates to A, and finally, Violet vibrates to the note of B. When there is a problem with a particular part of the anatomy, it can be treated quite effectively with the appropriate colour combined with the bija-mantra that corresponds to the chakra responsible for that area of the body. Although a sceptic may very well dismiss this concept as far-fetched, it is a method of treatment that needs to be tried before judged. Besides, this is one of the oldest methods of healing, and one that was favoured by colour therapists in ancient Egypt, although the mantras I am using were probably unknown to them.

Although the appropriate mantra may be used by itself to influence the affected part of the anatomy, the holistic approach is far more effective; that is, before we can treat the part, we must first consider the whole. For this reason the Bija-mantras need to be chanted in quick succession, over and over for at least ten minutes. Here's what you should do.

THE METHOD

- *The seven Bija-Mantras are, beginning at the base of the spine (which includes the feet up,) LAM, VAM, RAM, YAM, HAM,*

KSHAM (Don't sound the K) and finally OM.

- *For the best effect, learn the Bija-Mantras by Rote, sit on a straight backed chair with your eyes closed. Breathe rhythmically for a few minutes ensuring you are quite relaxed, and then simply chant the Bija-Mantras, beginning with LAM and concluding with OM.*

- *Repeat the chanting over and over again for ten minutes, longer if you feel inclined, and then relax.*

- *Once you have mastered the art of chanting, slow the whole process down and then repeat it all again, this time visualising the corresponding colours of each Bija-Mantra as you chant them.*

Although initially quite laborious, incredible results can be achieved in a very short space of time. Chanting is most certainly good for your health, particularly when it is combined with a little visualisation.

CHAPTER FOURTEEN

HEALING THROUGH THE AURA

Although the aura has been discussed at length in an earlier chapter, I would like to explore the application of healing through it, and take a look at how the aura may be used as a conduit for the healing force. Whilst it is true that disease is seen in the aura long before it becomes apparent in the body, it is equally as true that some diseases remain solely in the aura without ever infiltrating through to the physical body. If this is not addressed the individual is eventually worn down both mentally as well as physically, and then it becomes one of those rare health problems that can never be diagnosed. To a qualified medical practitioner this may sound ridiculously absurd, but from a mediumistic point of view it is something I have experienced many times, particularly where my own health is concerned.

Although not all disease originates in the aura, physical disease is reflected in the aura before it shows obvious symptoms in the body. Sometimes a disease may lie dormant in the cellular system for many years before actually erupting, and so this is where the aura becomes an extremely useful early warning diagnostic tool. Although those working in the field of medicine would probably regard treating disease through the aura as a 'New Age' notion, it is something that radiologist, Walter Kilner, successfully achieved with his aura screens at St Thomas' Hospital in the early part of the twentieth century. I have explained that the aura is best described as a vaporous mass of electromagnetic particles surrounding the human form, and that it interpenetrates the physical body as well as completely surrounding it. The aura of a healthy person is quite clean and compact, radiating evenly from the body with absolutely no spaces between the radiations. Although very colourful, the colours in the aura correspond with the individual's thoughts, feelings, worries, endeavours and even highlighting the food he or she has eaten. Although the aura of an unhealthy person creates the same colour phenomena, these are usually dull and lifeless, with noticeable fragmentations and breaks in the overall appearance of the subtle energy system. The healer should make every attempt to repair the fragmentations, and once this has been achieved, he or she should set about 'cleaning' the existing colours and infusing them with more vitality. This treatment usually takes it out of the healing practitioner, and so treatments should be limited to once or maybe twice a week. If you are seriously considering using healing treatment in this way, it is of little consequence if you are unable to actually 'see' the aura, as treatment is often as effective when the healer is guided intuitively through the healing process.

HEALING TREATMENT ONE

- *Seat the patient on a straight back chair, ensuring that he or she is quite relaxed with their eyes closed and their hands resting lightly on their lap.*
- *Ask them to breathe rhythmically for a few moments, making sure that the inhalations and exhalations are as evenly spaced as possible. In fact, gently talk them through the breathing process to relax him or her even more.*
- *Standing behind the patient, gently place your hands, one on each shoulder.*
- *Remain in that position, making every attempt to blend with the patient and attune your thoughts to theirs.*
- *Next, place both hands on top of the patient's head, side by side, palms down and fingers spread. Allow the hands to remain in that position until some heat has been created.*

- *Now, raise your hands approximately two inches above the head, and slowly move them down to the patient's waste, one either side.*
- *Once the waste has been reached, follow the same route slowly back to the top of the head. Allow your hands to remain there for a few moments, before repeating the same process again. In fact, repeat this procedure four or five times, more if you feel inclined.*
- *Now, move to the side of the patient and place your hands on his or her head as before, only this time, one hand on the forehead and one on the back of the head.*
- *After a few moments, raise your hands approximately two inches as before, and follow the same process from the side, stopping at the stomach and lower back. Follow the same route back to the forehead and back of the head.*
- *Repeat this process several times, and then begin shaking your hands vigorously as you move down the body.*

HEALING TREATMENT TWO

- *Pause for a few moments, standing behind the patient with your hands by your sides, and your eyes closed. Mentally see the patient in front of you, and attempt to attune your thoughts with them before moving on to the following treatment.*
- *Follow the same process as before, only this time, with your hands rigidly extended, make 'chopping' movements down the body, as though cutting off the rough edges of the individual's aura. Repeat this several times, before moving to the side of the patient.*
- *Finally, repeat the 'chopping' process several times from the side, and on the conclusion stand behind the patient with your hands one on either shoulder.*

Because the aura is composed of subtle energy, it is not necessary to actually make physical contact with the person. The chopping action encourages a more consistent flow of energy and helps to repair any breaks and fragmentations. A little visualisation helps with this part of the treatment. As already explained, because the treatment depletes the healing practitioner's own personal energy levels, the treatment should really only be applied once or twice a week at the most. To ensure that depleted energy levels are quickly restored, it is also a good idea for the healer to practise the following replenishing exercise.

REPLENISHING EXERCISE

- *Sit on a straight-back chair, making sure that the chest, neck and head are as nearly in a straight line as possible, and that your shoulders are thrown slightly back.*
- *Clasp your hands in front of you, across your stomach, with the tips of your thumbs touching.*
- *With your eyes closed, breathe-in a complete breath, pulling your thumbs apart, and visualising the in-coming breath as being coloured pink or coral.*
- *When the breath is complete, close your thumbs together once again, thus 'sealing' the tap, so to speak, and exhale, visualising the out-pouring breath as being coloured grey or even brown.*
- *Repeat this process several times for a feeling of invigoration.*

It is a good idea to conclude the above exercise by drinking a glass of freshly charged water. This hydrates the body and encourages the movement of prana in the major organs. The psychological effects of the above exercise are tremendous, and it is an ideal way of preparing the mind before going into a stressful situation, such as an interview for a job, or even when faced with something extremely traumatic. It also helps to lower stress levels by reducing the amount of adrenaline released into the body during an anxious or stressful period.

I have previously explained that the aura is also our prehistoric 'radar system', and is constantly scanning the surrounding environment for approaching danger. This process is relentless and is active regardless of whether or not we are mindful of it. When we are alone in an unfamiliar environment, our aura automatically extends in preparation for the detection of approaching danger. Although it does this quite unconsciously, it is not a sixth sense, but more a mechanism of defence. Your aura records all personal data pertaining to your health, psychological background, spiritual status, and even your dreams and aspirations. The electromagnetic materials of which the aura is comprised also encourage you to follow certain routes, and even help to attract into your life new people and conducive situations and conditions. It is an extremely sensitive medium through which energy is transmitted as well as drawn-in from the surrounding environment and other people. In fact, an oppressive, negative environment can deplete your aura just as easily as a negative individual. Because of a healer's sensitivity, he or she should always be prepared for such depletion, which can affect the aura both at a psychological as well as a spiritual level. Should you allow this depletion to persistently occur, then its holistic effect on the body will become apparent within time.

A healthy, well balanced diet accompanied by an adequate amount of daily exercise is of paramount importance when seriously considering dedicating your life to healing. I wish I had a pound for every time I have heard a healer say, 'The healing is nothing whatsoever to do with me. I am simply the instrument!' That may very well be, but the instrument really needs to be in good working order, healthy and finely tuned. A healer in poor health does not make a good channel for any sort of healing. An unhealthy healer can in some circumstances make the patient feel much worse, thus defeating the whole object of the exercise. The aura of an unhealthy healing practitioner is very often extremely fragmented and lacking in vitality. Persistently giving healing whilst in this poor state only suffices to make the health of the healer deteriorate even more. I cannot stress enough the importance of meditation to stabilise and focus the aura. Although meditation is nearly always practised to encourage altered states of consciousness, the disciplines of meditation may also be used to cleanse and strengthen the aura as well as clear your personal bioluminescence. The effects of meditation cover a broad psychological spectrum, and as well as encouraging a more consistent movement of energy in the aura, it also promotes calmness and serenity. As I have stressed all through the book, all meditation techniques should ideally begin and conclude with a short period of rhythmic breathing. This makes the mind quiet and prepares it for the process of meditation, and when you have finished it produces a sort of holistic 'washing' effect upon the aura, thus closing everything down, so to speak, bringing the mind back to reality. Apart from this rhythmic breathing is healing in itself by effectively moving prana through the blood and evenly distributing it to the major organs of the body. There is very little doubt that rhythmic breathing is an extremely effective tool and may even be used by the healing practitioner to direct his or her own healing energies to a patient, distance no problem.

As I have said in a previous chapter this technique of controlled breathing ,*Pranayama*, has been used successfully by yogi masters for thousands of years. It is a known fact that in the Western world the process of our breathing is greatly inefficient and is most probably the cause of many of our illnesses. Speaking as someone who has suffered since childhood with a serious lung condition, I know only too well the importance of correct breathing. For one thing the breathing process of the majority of people is extremely shallow and is controlled chiefly by the bellowing process of the upper chest area, as opposed to the diaphragm and stomach. On the inhalation of the breath the stomach should rise, and on the exhalation it should fall. Training yourself to breathe in this way encourages a more effective distribution of Prana throughout the bloodstream. Once this correct way of breathing has been fully mastered you can then introduce various degrees of measured counting into the breathing process. We have already given an example of this in an earlier chapter, but once you have learned the art of breath control, and have mastered the technique, the length of inhalations and exhalations may be increased. As I have already explained, Prana may be influenced and controlled by the mind, and may also be infused with the colour required for the healing process. This method may either be employed to draw the appropriate colour-infused Prana into your own system, (for the purpose of revital-isation) or it can quite easily be directed to another individual for the purpose of healing. As this book is primarily about healing, I have only touched upon the basic principles of Pranayama suffi-ciently to give you some understanding of the process of this sort of breathing. If this is a subject in which you are interested there are many books available, one of which is the highly recom-mended work by Hiroshi Motoyama, *THE THEORIES OF THE CHAKRAS*.

When endeavouring to heal through the aura, it must always be borne in mind that the electromagnetic atmosphere of another person is always accessed long before physical contact has been established. This also means that healing may be applied to a person's aura without them even being aware of what you are doing. A simple experiment will demonstrate this phenomenon. Next time you are sitting in a theatre, or even standing in a queue, simply focus your attention on someone a few feet in front of you, without making them aware of what exactly you are doing. Send the person you are focusing on the mental command to scratch their ear or head, or even to turn round to look at you. You will be surprised how quickly this will happen. This is a clear indication that you have the power within you to influence another person simply by directing your thoughts towards them, regardless of distance. Always remember, *within you there is more.*

CHAPTER FIFTEEN

THE SCIENCE OF THE ENDOCRINE SYSTEM

In our study of the effects of healing on the human organism, it must be borne in mind that before we can heal the part it is necessary to first consider the *whole*. This is the fundamental principle underlying the holistic approach to healing. I have already explained in a previous chapter that the human organism is an electromagnetic unit of immense power, appropriating, assimilating and releasing energy, and is contained within its own spectrum of light and colour. Therefore the efficiency of the body as a whole is to all intents and purposes dependent upon the individual parts of which the whole unit is comprised. Should a single part of the body cease to function effectively, then the efficiency of the whole unit is greatly impaired as a direct consequence. Although we have explored the subtle anatomy – the chakras - and the part they play in the spiritual evolution of consciousness, we must now make a detailed analysis of the physical counterparts of the chakras – the endocrine glands and nerve plexuses, and explore the integral part they play in the general health and well-being of the physical body.

The endocrine glands play an extremely important part in the holistic health of the body, and the overall personality of the individual is to some extent regulated by one or the other of these glands.

The endocrine glands are sometimes referred to as 'ductless' because they have no ducts and secrete their hormones directly into the bloodstream. These glands in fact collectively form the so-called endocrine system which directly corresponds with the chakra system, and vice versa. As I have already said, the overall health of the body is dependent upon the efficiency of the endocrine glands, and the inefficiency of one of these glands will impact upon the others.

The endocrine system is comprised of the pineal and the pituitary glands, located strategically in the cavity of the skull; the thyroid and parathyroid, situated near the larynx at the base of the neck; the thymus, situated strategically in the chest above the heart; the pair of adrenals (or suprarenals) topping the kidneys almost like tiny hoods; and the gonads of the male and female reproductory system. All the endocrine glands are closely related and supplement and depend upon each other. The healthy functioning of the endocrine glands is of paramount importance to the well-being of the individual, and the minute secretions of hormones from each are responsible for the development of the genius as opposed to the imbecile, or the restricted growth of the dwarf as opposed to the giant, or even the release of either happiness as opposed to sadness. In fact, the endocrine glands exert an incredible influence over the growth of our bodies and the development of the working of our minds, and in more ways than one really make us who and what we are. Their pervasive influence affects everything we do, and also not only helps to determine the shape of our body, but also affects the way we think and behave.

The pituitary gland is very often perceived as the most important gland, and has been described as the gland that 'gives the tune to all other glands,' which appear to be totally dependent on it. In fact, the pituitary gland encourages and controls the inner mobility and efficiency of the whole system and promotes and controls the growth of the body, glands and organs including sexual development. It supervises and maintains the efficient performance of the various structures and helps in the prevention of excessive fat accumulation. A happy uncomplicated individual without any obvious hang-ups is nearly always indicative of a healthy, active and normal working pituitary gland.

The pineal gland is a pine-shaped body deep within the brain. This is usually larger in a child than it is in the adult, and marginally more developed in the female than it is in the male. The pineal gland appears to harmonise the internal environment, and supervises the development of the other glands, thus maintaining their synchronicity and polarity in relation to each other. The pathological condition of the pineal gland is believed to exert a strong influence over the sex glands and causes the premature development of the system as a whole. In the pineal gland's normal condition it promotes harmony and efficient functioning of the endocrine system.

The inner activity in the endocrine system is controlled by the thyroid gland, ensuring that the tissues are fully active with no water retention, and that there is no densification of bones. The general condition of the thyroid is responsible for whether a person is very active or lethargic, tired or energetic, alert or depressed. The thyroid also controls the development and function of the sex organs.

The overall stability of the functioning within our body is to some extent influenced by the parathyroid glands, which maintains metabolic equilibrium by supervising the distribution and activity of calcium and phosphorus in our system. The healthy performance of these glands maintains constant balance of calcium and phosphorus, resulting in poise and tranquillity.

When puberty is reached the actual size and importance of the thymus gland is reduced, as the part it previously played in supervising natural growth and development should have by then been successfully achieved. The shrinking process of the thymus gland ensures that the natural adjustment of the individual is not impaired in anyway whatsoever.

The inner vitality and energy is encouraged by the adrenal glands, with a relentless drive to action, perception, activity, courage and vigour. The adrenal glands encourage oxygenation of the bloodstream, intensifying this process with revitalised power.

The phenomenon of attraction to the opposite sex is largely the result of healthy gonads of the male and female reproductory system, whose primary function is to maintain that attraction by encouraging the personality to radiate with confidence and self-assurance. The release of hormones from the gonads encourages inner warmth in the system ensuring that flexibility is maintained and that the overall health and vitality continues.

The overall health and vitality of the endocrine system is to some extent maintained by the regular distribution of the life-force – prana – throughout the entire organism. A little under-standing of the way in which this life force permeates the subtle channels should enable every healing practitioner to more effec-tively supervise the healing treatment, and thus facilitate the whole process more efficiently.

Although we have explored the chakra system and its function in a previous chapter, it is now necessary to make a detailed analysis of exactly how it corresponds with the endocrine glands and nerve plexuses, thus giving you a deeper comprehension of the effects of healing on the whole person.

I have explained that not only is prana the subtle agent through which the life of the body is sustained, but that it is also the principle largely responsible for the integration of the cells into a *whole*. In other words, prana is the metaphysical binding force of the universe, integrating the individual parts into a whole. Once prana begins to withdraw from the physical body as a consequence of the ageing process, the skin becomes fragile and loses its elasticity, causing it to wrinkle and fade. As prana also encourages and supervises mobility, as we age the movement of our limbs is gradually impaired and we have diffi-culty in getting around. Eventually prana can no longer circulate efficiently throughout the body, and so we die. The complete withdrawal of prana from the body causes its gradual disinte-

gration, forcing the cells to run amok. However, upon disinte-
gration, the individual cells comprised by the body take with
them sufficient prana to enable them to form new combinations.
So we can see that even in the process of death the residue of
prana relentlessly perpetuates life. Nothing can ever die! In
saying this however, nothing in this world of form is permanent.
Everything is in perpetual vibration, and within the confines of
that vibratory cycle a constant rhythm is maintained, pulsating
through the universe and resounding through every cell of our
being. The swing of the planets around the sun, the rise and fall
of the sea, and the perpetual beating of our heart; everything is
constantly vibrating with a certain rhythm. Rhythm in fact
pervades the entire universe. The atoms of which the physical
body is composed are as much an integral part of the continuous
rhythmical cycle; and so when we step outside of this cycle
disharmony immediately manifests in our lives, either as disease
in the body or the mind, or just as a sequence of insurmountable
difficulties in our life. A healthy body and mind can only be
maintained when there is inner harmony, thus allowing the body,
mind and spirit to resonate with the universal rhythm, or
universal mind as it is known in eastern mysticism. A healing
practitioner should be able to encourage such harmonious vibrations in the body of someone who is 'out of tune' so to speak, thus
allowing health and harmony to be completely restored.

Mentally encouraging the individual organs
Although the very notion of actually communicating with the
individual cells and organs of a patient's body might sound
extremely bizarre to the sceptic, it is perhaps one of the oldest
and most effective forms of healing, and one that was favoured
by yogic mystics of antiquity. The process is quite simple and
involves dialogue between the healer and the various parts of his
or her body. The healing practitioner mentally encourages the
distribution of the vital force through the individual endocrine

glands, ensuring that each one is revitalised. Although this healing process involves a little visualisation, the primary part of the treatment is the mental dialogue. Simply mentally pass on to the glands the desire for them to be healthy and full of vigour and vitality. The healer needs to spend some time mentally scanning the patient's body, and willing the individual parts to integrate harmoniously with the whole. Once you are satisfied that sufficient time has been spent on the endocrine glands, you can then direct your attention to the diseased part of the body, thus applying the same treatment. This method of healing should take at least an hour, so it is vitally important that the patient is reposed in a comfortable, relaxed position. Although this method of healing requires some effort on the practitioner's part, the benefits are quite remarkable and may be seen almost immediately on the conclusion of the treatment. After the treatment you should ensure that the patient is well hydrated. It is a good idea to charge a glass of water by pouring it from one vessel to another, backward and forward for a few moments, until the water sparkles and seems to come alive.

CHAPTER SIXTEEN

GROUP HEALING

The power created by a group of healing practitioners can be quite astounding, particularly when the healing force is focused on one individual. Two of the most powerful processes of group healing are *Battery Healing* and what I call, *The Spiralling Mantra*, both of which create and harness an incredible force that can be used in the treatment of all sorts of illnesses. First of all let us explore the concept of Battery Healing and how that may be used in a small group. I have explained in an earlier chapter that the physical body is an electromagnetic unit of incredible energy. This electromagnetic unit is constantly discharging and drawing energy to it, and whether or not you are actually aware of the subtle process, your personal energies have a profound effect on all those with whom you come into contact. This is one of the primary reasons you occasionally feel a little depleted when in the presence of someone who is not feeling too well. They however, may suddenly 'pick up' after being with you for any length of time, leaving you feeling out of sorts. However, this depletion is not permanent, and as soon as he or she has left your company, your depleted energy levels are quickly restored. Once you fully understand the concept of energy transference you should then begin to see just how easily you can restore the vitality in another person, a process which is either performed with or without his or her knowledge. Battery Healing is simply a healing treatment in which individual energies are combined and focused on one individual.

For the process you will require six people, preferably three males and three females, although this is not absolutely necessary.

THE METHOD

- *Seat the person to be treated on a straight back chair, with his or her hands resting lightly on the lap, right palm up, left palm down.*
- *Seat the healers in a semicircle from either side of the patient.*
- *The healer on the right side of the patient should take his or her hand in their left hand (palm down), and take the next healer's hand in their right hand, (palm up).*
- *The next person should follow the same procedure, and so on until the semi-circle is concluded, and the final person completes the battery by taking the patient's hand, which is palm up.*
- *The treatment should commence with some slow, rhythmic breathing, which should be supervised by the person in charge.*
- *On the leader's instructions, inhale a slow and complete breath, and when the word is given, the group should exhale slowly, visualising the out-pouring breath as a stream of intense white light, moving round the semi-circle in a clockwise motion, filling the patient with the full force and vitality of the exhaled energy.*
- *Continue this process for ten minutes, longer if necessary, and then the group should relax with their eyes closed.*
- *It is important to maintain the hand connection, and only release this when the treatment is finished.*
- *It also helps the precipitation of the healing force if the patient joins in the process of rhythmic breathing.*
- *On the conclusion of the treatment the patient usually feels disorientated and sometimes a little tired. As with all healing treatments it is a good idea for the person receiving the treatment to drink a tumbler of charged water.*

The battery method of healing has a holistic effect upon the individual, and applied on a regular basis encourages the body to normalise itself. It is an ideal tonic for anyone who is feeling under the weather or out of sorts, and can even be used on an individual who is recovering from a serious illness.

Some years ago I created the *Spiralling Mantra* for use in a fairly large healing group. I called it this for reasons that will become apparent to you later on. It creates such power that everyone is affected, both those in the group and also those who observe the process from outside. The Spiralling Mantra is extremely effective in the revitalization of the chakra system, and has a profound effect upon the aura and subtle anatomy. It somehow energizes all the participants, and promotes alertness and sharpness of the senses.

THE SPIRALLING MANTRA

- *Form a circle (using chairs) with, if possible, males and females seated alternately. Should equal numbers of males and females not be present, don't worry; just seat them as best as you can.*
- *As with the battery method each person's left hand should be turned palm up, and their right hand palm down. Touch hands with person next to you, until the circuit has been formed, all around the circle.*
- *With eyes closed, the group should now spend five or ten minutes breathing slowly a deeply, maintaining a steady, even rhythm throughout the group.*
- *Begin to imagine a pulsating stream of pure white light passing around the circle, flowing from one person to the next, along the arms and through the hands.*
- *By now you should have noticed a difference in the room temperature. Group members may also begin to experience some tingling in their hands.*
- *The group should now begin to chant a specific mantra. Although most words with symbolic meaning will create energy when chanted rhythmically, the word to be used here is 'KSHAM'. The 'K' is silent in the word, so it should therefore be chanted as 'SHAM'. The word Ksham is a powerful mantra and*

is the one that is used to activate a release of the inherent qualities of Ajna, the brow chakra. However, the group should not chant the mantra exactly in unison, but should stagger it, leaving about one second between each person's intonation.

- *Group member one should commence chanting. Inhaling a deep breath he will chant the word Ksham on his exhalation, maintaining the sound until his breath has been fully expelled.*

- *One second after the first person begins chanting, the group member on his left, should then begin, chanting the mantra in the same way.*

- *One second after that person begins to chant, the person on his left should then commence chanting, and so on.*

- *Following this procedure the sound of the chanting will travel clockwise around the circle, each person chanting the mantra in turn.*

- *The voices should be sounded as loudly as possible, always remembering to keep your hands in the same position throughout the process of chanting.*

- *Each person should continue chanting until all the breath has been fully expelled, and then wait until the sound has completed the circuit and returned to them. At this point, another deep breath should be inhaled, and expelled one second after the person on the right has begun to sound the mantra.*

- *The chanting should be maintained for ten minutes – longer if possible – and then, on a given instruction, allow the chanting to fade into silence.*

- *When the group has fallen silent each person should remain still, allowing the hands to remain in the same position, with their eyes closed, and allow the energy to circulate from one to the other, around the circle.*

- *The effects of the Spiralling Mantra are quite spectacular, and do have a remarkable effect upon all involved.*

The Spiralling Mantra needs to be practised until everyone

involved feels comfortable with the process and fully understands what it is trying to achieve. Once the technique has been mastered, a patient may be sat in the centre of the circle to receive its full healing benefits. The patient should sit with his or her eyes closed and hands resting on the lap all through the process. He or she should remain in that position until the exercise has been concluded, at which point each member of the circle should stand up one at a time, briefly touching the patient's shoulder, thus discharging the residue of the force to conclude the treatment.

The Spiralling Mantra encourages the creation and focus of an incredible force primarily for the purpose of healing. It can be created and discharged in the healing treatment of one or more individuals, or it can be released towards a particular country or even a nation stricken by famine or war. Practised regularly, the Spiralling Mantra also has the effect of cleansing the atmosphere of a location where there is paranormal disturbance.

Cautionary note: When energy is created in this way it cannot be left, and must be discharged through a positive healing process.

Some healers prefer to heal with a partner as opposed to practising healing alone. This will only work effectively when there is a special affinity between the two practitioners. Should this not be the case then adverse negative energies may be created, affecting both the patient and the healers.

Contrary to what many interested in healing believe, simply wanting to be a healer is not sufficient. As with mediums who are born and not made, the potential for healing has to be present. Certain forms of psychic healing may be developed by almost anyone, to some greater or lesser degree; but Spiritual Healing is something quite different, and really develops of its own accord in those who possess the potential. In all cases, a strong desire to help others needs to be present. This desire is very often supported by an overwhelming feeling of compassion. Without compassion healing will simply not work.

CHAPTER SEVENTEEN

ATTUNEMENT AND TECHNIQUE

The longer you are involved in the process of healing, the more your sensitivity to everything will become heightened. Interacting with people who to all intents and purposes, are 'out of tune' will in time increase your awareness of the vibratory tones of a person's body, and you will most probably find yourself guided instinctively to a particular part of the anatomy, whether or not this is the part of the body that is causing the problem. Experience will frequently enable a good doctor to instinctively detect illness in the patient, very often without any consideration of the symptoms. Many medical practitioners become accustomed to the actual smell of disease, and are able to make a diagnosis simply by identifying a specific odour. Although healers should never offer a diagnosis for a health condition, with the use of the same 'smelling' process, some healers become acquainted with certain illnesses, which will guide them intuitively to the part of the body where healing is required.

It may surprise many people to learn that all diseases do have their own particular odours, and many doctors rely on their sense of smell as a diagnostic tool. When treating disease on a regular basis, this ability develops quite naturally, and may then be used in your work as a healer. It is believed that certain diseases do have distinctive odours, caused by a change in metabolic processes associated with the patient's condition. Victorian doctors were very often able to identify arsenic poisoning because of the odour of garlic. A fruity smell on the breath would be an indication that either the person was a diabetic or was starving.

Some illnesses possess very distinctive odours and may easily be identified. For example, German Measles apparently smells like plucked feathers; Scrofula, which is a form of tuberculosis, smells like stale beer. Typhoid has the distinctive smell of baking bread, and Yellow Fever has the overwhelming smell of a butcher's shop. An experienced surgeon will always be able to identify bacterial infection by the smell of the patient's bandages. A musty, damp cellar smell can be an indication of an infected wound. Experience alone will encourage the development of your sense of 'smell' when administering healing, and although in time the different odours of illness will not be as apparent to you, they will still influence your senses and continue to intuitively guide you. It is a known psychological fact that obnoxious smells become less noticeable in time, especially when you are frequently exposed to them. Even though this is the case your ability to instinctively sense disease through odour will continue to develop. The process of healing has a holistic effect upon the faculties, and develops in the same way as mediumistic skills develop through application and use.

Dogs and cats home-in to their sick owners in very much the same way. Dogs more than cats are able to monitor molecular changes in their owner's atmosphere, and always appear to gravitate to the part of the anatomy that is causing the problem. It is now a proven scientific fact that dogs and cats have a profound effect upon their owner's health. No sooner do they detect that their owner is unwell when the dog releases a subtle energy into the atmosphere. This somehow encourages the release of endorphins (the body's natural pain killer) in the brain, encouraging the dog's owner to feel psychologically and physically better..

Healing has been practised through antiquity. Up until as late as the eighteenth century in Britain, some people believed that the monarch's so-called 'Royal Touch' could cure all manner of ailments, and would go to any lengths to be touched by the King or Queen. Today it is a well known scientific fact that touching does have specific value in relieving pain or discomfort of any kind. The recovery of a child after it has fallen is hastened by the soothing touch of its mother. Science however offers its own reasons why touch sooths pain. Scientists in fact believe that stimulation of the nerves through the process of touch or rubbing interrupts the signals received by the pain receptors, thus alleviating the full sensation of pain impulses on the brain's cerebral cortex. This does not explain why some people possess the ability to ease discomfort and pain in another person, and some do not. Other scientific research has shown that like dogs and cats, some people are able to discharge a subtle energy that can affect the human organism, thus promoting feelings of calmness and well-being. It must be said however, that there have been cases where a person simply has not responded to a healer, even though the healer's abilities were known to be quite powerful. There has to be some sort of affinity between patient and healer who must form a relationship in which both feel comfortable with each other. A healing relationship sometimes has to be worked at, and mental barriers frequently have to be overcome by one of the healing practitioners, who may, on rare occasions, feel a little resentment for the person to whom he or she is going to administer healing. This may come as a great shock to some people. However, I have seen this on numerous occasions where the healer has had an obvious dislike for the person who has consulted them for healing. Even when the healer is overwhelmed with a feeling of resentment, for whatever the reason, not making the resentment apparent will still defeat the object of the exercise, which is after all to promote feelings of well-being in the patient. Healers are human after all; and think of them what we will, they are still subject to the same human failings as everyone else. Overcoming these is perhaps not the easiest of tasks, which is why meditation should be integrated into your healing development programme. Meditation may not remove any resentment you may have for the occasional person who consults you for healing, but it will certainly help to encourage in the long term the development of inner-calm and tolerance – prerequisites for a good healing practitioner. However, it must be borne in mind that what meditation suits one person may not suit another. It may even be necessary for you to create your own meditation technique. At least 15 minutes of your day should be devoted to a period of contemplation and meditation. During the contemplative period I would suggest you make a detailed analysis of all your faults. Should you be harbouring any feelings of animosity towards anyone, analyse these in your contemplation and make every endeavour to eradicate them completely. In the transmission of healing it is important that the healing force is in no way restricted by negative emotions. See them for what they are. Do not ignore or suppress your faults, deal with them each time you enter a period of contemplation. Negative feelings in anyway whatsoever will inhibit your healing ability, and will eventually affect you emotionally. Remember the precept quoted in an earlier chapter: *'Curses and Blessings Come Home to Roost.'*

Precede and conclude all meditation exercises with a period of slow rhythmic breathing. This prepares the mind for meditation, and also closes everything down on its conclusion. Should you have difficulty in holding the concentration for any length of time, the easiest meditation method is candle scrying. This requires very little effort and simply involves the process of gazing.

- *Create a background of some quiet atmospheric music, and burn some pleasant incense to set the mood.*
- *Light a candle and place it on a table as near to eye level as possible.*
- *Simply gaze at the flame without blinking, and resist the temptation to look away even for a moment.*

- *When your eyes begin to tear and you can no longer look at the flame; close your eyes and place the palms of your hands over them, applying a little pressure to the eyeball.*
- *Within moments the after-image will appear in your mind's eye. Hold the image for as long as you possibly can, and when it becomes fragmented and begins to fade, open your eyes and return your gaze to the flame, and repeat the process.*
- *In fact, repeat the gazing process three times, and then relax.*
- *Conclude the exercise with a little rhythmic breathing.*

Candle scrying promotes serenity and encourage concentration. Although strictly speaking this is not meditation, it is an excellent tool with which to cultivate the senses. Used over a period of time it cultivates a heightened sense of awareness, and helps the development of sensory perception, thus encouraging the release of latent psychic skills.

CHAPTER EIGHTEEN

INTUITION, IMAGINATION AND THE LAW OF ATTRACTION

In my workshops I have always used the word 'Intuition' as an umbrella term to cover a broad spectrum of psychic and mental skills. Although we all possess intuition to some greater or lesser degree, research has shown that only a minority of us actually use it in our everyday life. Nonetheless, intuition may be developed with use, and may also be cultivated to such a high degree as to become just as reliable as any of our other five recognised senses. Although imagination is somewhat different, it is nonetheless something we all seem to take for granted, even though this is not always used to its fullest potential. The imaginative powers of some individuals can be so realistically powerful that it can create and release extremely vivid images that can either bring about fear and dread to the individual or extreme feelings of ecstasy and joy. Intuition and imagination combined becomes an extremely powerful tool, not only where the process of healing is concerned, but also when connecting with other universal forces, such as that of the *law of attraction*.

THE UNIVERSAL LAW OF ATTRACTION

Today it has become quite fashionable to refer to the universe as the *Great Giver*; and there is no end of books explaining how we can call upon the universe for all the things we require. The Law of Attraction is by no means new, and has always been an integral part of eastern esoteric traditions. An understanding of the Law of Attraction can empower you and enable you to gain greater control of your life. In an earlier chapter I quoted an ancient precept, '*Thoughts crystallise into habit and habit solidifies into* circumstances.' This in some way explains how the way we think is the way we are; and in response to the way we think will nature always conspire to lead us into a situation whereby our thoughts and desires may be gratified. Thoughts are living things; the stronger our thoughts the longer they will persist in the atmosphere. The longer they persist, the more chance they have of bringing into our lives conditions of a similar nature. This is the Law of Attraction. The Law of Attraction will bring to us the things we fear as well as the things we desire, and so an understanding of this universal process will make us much more in control of our lives. Only when we change the way we think will our circumstances then change. By training your mind to think in a specific pure and positive way, without malice, jealousy, hate or greed, will your body respond by becoming healthy, strong and pure. By diligently searching for the hidden laws that regulate your life, will you then become a spiritual being of the universe, wise and in control of everyday circumstances and events. It is absolutely true that men do not attract that which they want, but that which they are! For the universe is never wrong; and when its laws are fully understood, everything else goes right! A man's character comes about as a consequence of the way he thinks; and when his thoughts do not harmonise with the universe, one problem after another arises in his life. It was once said: 'To desire is to obtain; to aspire is to achieve.' It is so true that the dreamer of the almost impossible shall in time realise his dream. Your vision of a life full of happiness and success will eventually become a reality, as will all the things you fear and dread. This is the Law of Attraction – a law that is both right and just!

You may wonder what the Universal Law of Attraction has to do with healing. Well, it has more to do with healing than you realise. A healer needs some understanding of the universe and the way in which it orders things in our lives. It's well known in history that the great King Canute tried to hold back the tide. He could not of course, for the only way to conquer nature is by *obedience*. When we obey nature we can then choose from her boundless store the forces that serve our purpose. As a healer you need to work with nature and not try to control it. Once you fully understand the way the Universal Law of Nature actually works, you will then see that nothing is beyond your reach, and everything that happens truly happens under your control and because you have called it into your life. In fact, everything that actually goes wrong in your life is the result of ignorance, and is really due to the working of laws whose presence was unknown or overlooked. You will always reap what you sow, not because you are being punished for the things you have done wrong, but because the effect must always follow the cause. Theologians have always taught that we are punished for our sins. However, the higher teachings inform us that we are not in any way punished for the things we do wrong, but that we are punished by our own ignorance and the act of doing wrong itself.

Once you have learned to work with the universe, and have acknowledged that the universe is right; it will then present to you all the things it knows you to be!

IMAGINATION

To some extent imagination involves images passing through the consciousness. The image-making faculty of the brain plays an extremely important part in the transmission of the healing force, and is an effective tool for conveying healing at great distances. When in close proximity, use of the imagination becomes even more powerful in the administration of healing and can overwhelm a patient with feelings of strength, power and well-being. A mistake that is frequently made by healers when using imagery to convey healing is to mentally 'see' the patient as he or she actually is, in a state of sickness, and not as they should be, completely well and recovered from illness.

During the process of healing *imagination* supports *intuition* perfectly, and combined they become a powerful and extremely effective healing tool. I have known some healers to simply place their hands on the patient and to talk all through the treatment. They usually offer the excuse that the actual *healing* has nothing whatsoever to do with them and that they are merely the 'channel'. I find this a somewhat crass excuse; and although the statement about them being the channel is correct, in my opinion the healing practitioner needs to interact and help to keep that channel open. This involves a certain quietness and to keep the mind quite passive. There is very little doubt that the healing force may be helped somewhat with a little encouragement from the healer. With a little help from the imagination the healing force may be given wings almost; and although there is no necessity for the healer to actually apply his or her hands to the troubled part of the anatomy, with the use of intuition the healing force can be directed more effectively to the appropriate part of the body where the healing is required.

COMMENTS ABOUT PSYCHIC
DEVELOPMENT

It has been said that *Spiritual Healing* is the 'highest' form of mediumship, as it involves the extremely arduous process of establishing a connection with the *'higher-self'*. In this regard I suppose one could say that the actual development process of healing requires exactly the same approach and discipline as is required with the cultivation of mediumship.

Psychic development is nonetheless a mental process involving specific exercises to cultivate the faculties, with the sole intention of developing heightened states of awareness and sensory perception. Although all the techniques explored in this book may be used to develop such metaphysical abilities as Clairvoyance, Clairaudience and Clairsentience, and other heightened intuitive skills, they can just as effectively be employed to enhance the quality of your life and to help you exert a more positive control over it. As I have previously said elsewhere in the book, just as the body can be exercised to increase its strength and power, so too can the mind be trained to improve its overall efficiency and performance. Should your interest be primarily in the metaphysical advantages of the exercises given in the book, you must bear in mind that whilst everybody possesses psychic abilities potentially, to some greater or lesser degree, this is most certainly not the case where mediumistic healing skills are concerned. Although somewhat of a cliché, mediums are in fact born and not made, and a mediumistic ability may only be encouraged when there is latent potential present.

Although mediumistic abilities do have a tendency to be genetic, they can on rare occasions be precipitated as a result of a traumatic experience, such as an accident or illness, or even in very rare cases, through the emotional aftermath of bereavement.

Mediumistic tendencies very often follow the female genetic line, and regardless of what you believe, mediumistic skills by themselves are far from normal, and only become apparent because of biological and neurological changes, resulting from the transmutation of hormones and other chemicals in the endocrine glands and nerve plexuses. A healing skill involves much more than the simple process of the 'laying on of hands', and compassion is most certainly a prerequisite when embarking upon the path of healing. During the actual process of true Spiritual Healing, the practitioner appears to 'pass on' to the patient much more than subtle waves of energy and the warmth of the physical touch. Something other than these obvious *things* transpire during the application of healing, and it is not uncommon for the patient to remark upon an overwhelming sense of peace and calm having been experienced during the treatment. Although science is a little vague in its attempt to assess the process of Spiritual Healing, the scientific interest in the actual phenomena of all types of healing is relentless and so we must conclude that there is much more to the metaphysical aspects of healing that is perhaps beyond the parameters of traditional scientific calculations.

As I have briefly explained in an early part of the book, man's subtle energies are controlled to all intents and purposes by an intricate system of minute transformer-like units, (or vortices of energy) called 'Chakras', whose function is to control, modify and distribute the in-pouring 'universal' energy to the corresponding organs of the physical body, thus maintaining the individual's equilibrium and balance. Just as the smooth running of an automobile will be affected by the malfunctioning of one of its engine parts, so too can the effectiveness of the healing process be inhibited by inactivity in one or more of the essential chakras. And so, just like an automobile, the chakra system should be regularly overhauled to maintain its performance and efficiency. A daily programme of meditation will ensure that the subtle anatomy is maintained and that the healing practitioner's personal energies are consistent. During my workshops I always explore various 'power–breathing' techniques with a look at how these can be integrated into a healer's training programme. As we have seen earlier, such breathing methods are also effective in the transference of energy to another individual, primarily for the purpose of healing. When embarking upon the path of healing always keep in mind the biblical precept, *'Physician heal thyself'*, as in my opinion it is vitally important that the health of the healing practitioner is always maintained. I would also like to add to the above precept something my own mother always used to say to me 'A healthy mind makes a healthy body!' There is far more truth in this than you might realise.

CONCLUSION

Healing has been practised in one form or another through antiquity, but it is really only through biblical accounts of the healing by Jesus that the majority of people have come to attribute it primarily to religious ceremonies, dismissing anyone who gives healing with little or no religious intent. I have always believed that what is in the heart is more important than anything, and if the intention is good and well-meaning it will work, regardless of whether or not one is religious.

This book is primarily to give you some ideas of what and what not to do, and it is not necessary to use every exercise and method I have given. However, I would suggest that meditation should always be integrated into your training programme, and as long as you devote a little part of your day to meditation, how you do this is not that important.

Although it may be your intention to eventually give healing alone, initially it is often a good idea to work with other like-minded people. Apart from everything else this helps you to overcome the lack of confidence, (so common in the early stages of development) and allows other people to offer an opinion about your ideas and techniques. In any case, experimentation is important when endeavouring to develop the gift of healing, and working with like-minded people also gives you the opportunity to experiment with your skills with some confidence.

If you are seriously considering setting yourself up as a healer, whether professionally or in a small way, you will need to have some form of insurance to protect you. It is often more beneficial to become a member of a recognised healing body such as the National Federation of Spiritual Healers, or some similar organisation. After you have served the obligatory probationary period, you are automatically entered on their register of healers and legally covered under their insurance policy, usually up to the sum of £1,000,000. If you prefer to retain your autonomy you would be wise to seek the appropriate insurance cover. This would safeguard you against any accusations or unreasonable claims. In any case, a healer is always advised never to give healing to a member of the opposite sex unaccompanied. Common sense should always be used when giving healing, and a healing session should be structured and presented in an extremely professional way. When creating a healing clinic it is a good idea also to play some soothing, atmospheric music. This not only creates the correct ambience, extremely essential when healing is taking place, but it will also relax those to whom healing is being given.

I would like to take this opportunity in wishing you well in your aspirations and healing endeavours, and to remind you of the ancient precept: 'The thousand mile journey begins with the single step.' Once you have taken that first step, you can rest assured that your life will never be the same again.

AYNI
BOOKS

Ayni Books, publishes complementary and alternative approaches to health, healing and well-being, following a holistic model.